For my grandmother, Pauline Wills

Contents

The Mermaid Craft Book

Magical Makes for Your Inner Mermaid

Marianne Thompson

summersdale

THE MERMAID CRAFT BOOK

An Hachette UK Company
www.hachette.co.uk

Summersdale Publishers Ltd
Part of Octopus Publishing Group Limited
Carmelite House
50 Victoria Embankment
LONDON
EC4Y 0DZ
UK

www.summersdale.com

Printed and bound in China

ISBN: 978-1-78783-223-7

Substantial discounts on bulk quantities of Summersdale books are available to corporations, professional associations and other organizations. For details contact general enquiries: telephone: +44 (0) 1243 771107 or email: enquiries@summersdale.com.

Disclaimer

Crafting tools should be used carefully on an appropriate work surface. Always follow the manufacturer's guidelines when using craft materials with specific instructions and, if you have sensitive skin, protect your hands with rubber gloves when working with dyes, glues or paints. Little mermaids should always be supervised when crafting, and adults should always carry out the instructions which require the use of sharp or heated tools.

Introduction

Mermaids love sparkly trinkets and pretty treasures – they just can't seem to stop collecting them! If you are a mermaid and you're in need of some shimmering curiosities for your underwater grotto, or glamorous accessories for your festival wardrobe, flick your fins and dive into this book. You will discover a raft of beautiful aquatic crafts and magical mermaid makes – perfect for both grown-up and little mermaids alike. Whether you are a crafting beginner, or have been making for many moons, there is something for everyone living the mermaid life.

Note: Where equivalent imperial measurements have been included, they have been rounded up or down to the nearest unit, for the sake of practicality.

Crafting responsibly

Mermaids love the ocean and all the creatures within it, so, where possible, make environmentally friendly choices when selecting craft materials: use biodegradable or edible glitter, buy responsibly sourced shells rather than take them from beaches and recycle old materials like ribbons or fabric. Second-hand shops can be excellent places to find beads or threads and are often a good way of sourcing craft materials inexpensively.

A Mermaid's Toolkit

Many of the crafts within this book specify some specialist art materials you may not have used before. See the list below for a few helpful hints on what to buy and how to craft with some of these materials.

Two-part epoxy glue

Two-part epoxy glue is a strong, durable adhesive suitable for bonding materials like metal, ceramic, glass and most plastics. This glue comes in two tubes which must be mixed according to the manufacturer's instructions (usually equal quantities of each part). Most brands of epoxy glue will have a few different options for setting time, ranging from a few seconds to several hours. Epoxy glue is available from art and craft shops, but you can also find it online or in DIY stores.

Two-part epoxy clay

Useful for sculpting and making repairs to ceramics or metals, two-part epoxy clay is a durable, self-hardening clay which can be drilled, carved or sanded once set. This clay comes in two packets and must be mixed according to the manufacturer's instructions (usually equal quantities of each part). Once the two parts have been mixed, the clay will bond to most surfaces (even glass and plastics), can be smoothed with water and will set within an hour of mixing – even underwater! Epoxy clays are widely available online or in art and craft shops.

Polymer clay

This type of clay is non-air-drying and must be baked in an oven at a low temperature to harden. Polymer clays come in a huge variety of colours and can be mixed to create new shades. The clay requires kneading before use; a process often called "conditioning", which softens up the clay and makes it easier to sculpt. Different brands can differ in firmness, so conditioning time may vary. Polymer clay is widely available in art and craft shops or online.

Jewellery tools

There are a variety of small pliers specifically for jewellery making: cutting pliers will snip through jewellery findings and metal wires, flat-nosed pliers are useful for bending wires or opening small metal rings and round-nosed pliers are used for making loops.

Jewellery findings

Small metal bits and bobs such as loops or hooks which are used to create pieces of jewellery. Jewellery findings are available in craft or beading shops, but you will likely find the most variety online. Some examples used in this book are:

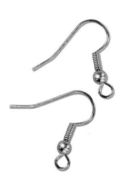

Clamshell bead tips

Ball headpins

Earring posts/ hooks/hoops

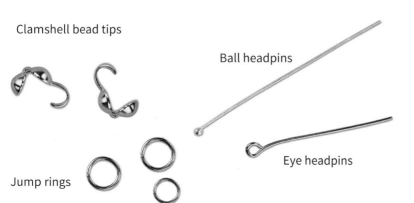

Eye headpins

Jump rings

Clasps

Glue gun

Glue guns are excellent for paper or card crafts which need to be glued quickly. You can purchase both "cold melt" and "hot melt" glue guns from art, craft and stationery shops.

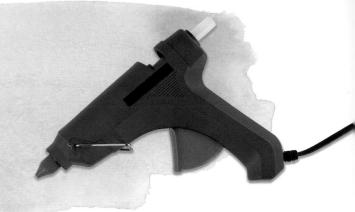

Acrylic paint

This paint is fast drying with high-density colour and can be easily found in art shops. It can come in a variety of thicknesses and can be diluted with water. It is best used on paper, card or canvas, but can also be used to paint stones or shells. Once dry, it has a smooth, plastic-like feel and is waterproof.

White (PVA) craft glue

This glue is suitable for bonding paper, card and wood and can come in a variety of thicknesses. Available in stationery shops, art shops, or online, this glue goes by many common names: school glue, craft glue, paper glue and PVA glue.

Biodegradable glitter

There are an increasing variety of edible, dissolvable and biodegradable glitters now available online or in craft, beauty and baking shops. If shopping online, always check that the product description is accurate, as some unsuitable products may turn up in your search results.

Shells and pebbles

Craft shops and garden centres are great places to source attractive shells and smooth river pebbles. You could also try asking at a supermarket deli for discarded scallop, cockle or oyster* shells.

*Warning. It is strongly advised not to drill into or cut oyster shells; the fine dust that is created is extremely toxic when inhaled as it hardens and turns to glass inside the lungs.

Soap base

"Melt and pour" soap bases are an ideal introduction to soap making as they are safer and easier to use in comparison to traditional soap-making techniques. If you are layering several colours, always remember to spray each layer with IPA alcohol to prevent the soap from splitting apart when sliced. Soap bases, essential oils and colourings are usually available in craft shops but are also widely available online.

Wax

Wax can be purchased in pellets or flake form ready to melt down and pour.

Ocean Fashion

*All the latest looks,
fresh from the reef!*

Scallop Shell Shirt

Sometimes it is just that little bit too chilly on the beach to wear your favourite shell bra, but don't worry; you can still wear your seashells on your T-shirt!

Materials:

- 2 pieces of card (0.5 mm thick), approx. 30 x 21 cm (12 x 8 ½ in.)
- Roll of double-sided sticky tape
- White cotton T-shirt or vest top (man-made fibres may not absorb fabric paint so well)
- Scrap card (2 mm thick), trimmed to fit snugly inside the T-shirt
- 25 ml (1 fl. oz) pot of "stay soft" pink fabric paint
- 25 ml (1 fl. oz) pot of "stay soft" purple fabric paint

Equipment:

- Pencil
- Ruler
- Craft knife
- Cutting mat
- Small sponge
- Palette for paint
- 2 pieces of plain cotton fabric, large enough to cover the T-shirt (you could use 2 tea towels)
- Iron and ironing board

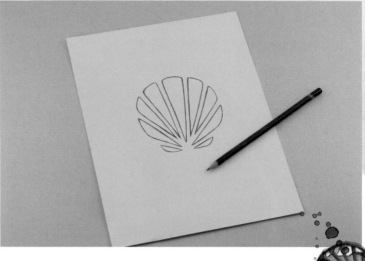

1 Draw a simple 10 cm (4 in.) diameter segmented shell onto one of the pieces of 30 x 21 cm (12 x 8 ½ in.) card. You may want to adjust the size of the shell by a few centimetres to suit the size of your T-shirt, or enlarge the template on page 157 to your desired size. Leave at least 4 mm between the sections of the shell; if these areas are too narrow, the shell will be difficult to cut out.

2 Cut out the middle sections of the shell using a craft knife and cutting mat. To make a second stencil, use the first as a guide to draw an identical shell shape onto another piece of 30 x 21 cm (12 x 8 ½ in.) card. Cut out the sections of the second stencil in the same way.

Trim small strips of double-sided sticky tape to fit around the edges of one stencil. You will need to stick the tape as closely to the edges as possible, as if there are any gaps the fabric paint may run underneath the stencil.

Iron the T-shirt to remove any creases and then slip the piece of thick cardboard inside, ensuring the card is beneath the area of fabric where you are going to paint. Not only will this create a smooth surface for sponging, it will also prevent the colour from seeping through to the back of the T-shirt.

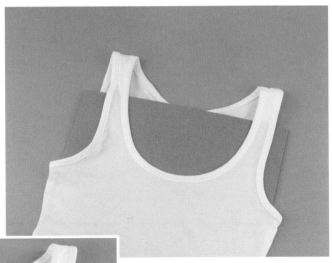

Peel off the surface of the double-sided tape. Place the stencil (sticky-side facing down) over one side of your T-shirt and smooth the card with your hand to make sure all areas of the stencil are stuck to the fabric.

Sponge pink fabric paint lightly over the stencil. Try not to over-saturate the T-shirt with paint or the colour may start to seep along the fibres of the fabric.

While the pink paint is still wet, use a clean area of the sponge to dab a little purple paint over the bottom of the stencil. Using the leftover paint on the sponge, blend the colours into one another to create a gradient effect. Don't worry if the purple looks blotchy, this can be remedied by sponging a small amount of pink paint back over the top to further mix the colours.

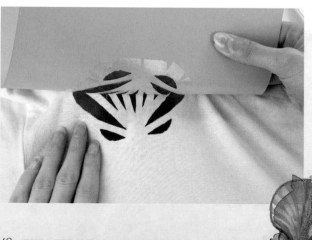

When the paint is completely dry, slowly peel the stencil off the T-shirt. Don't be tempted to pull too quickly or sharply as this may stretch the fabric.

Mermaid Tip:

Always check the washing instructions for your chosen brand of fabric paint. If in doubt, gently hand-wash painted garments in cool water to preserve the colour.

9

Use the second stencil to repeat the same sponging process (Steps 5–8) for the second shell.

10

Most fabric paints require ironing on a medium–high heat to fix the colour, but always check the instructions for your chosen brand of paint. Place the painted area between two pieces of plain cotton before ironing; this will prevent the paint transferring onto the iron.

Mermaid Crown

Every princess needs a crown, and you are Queen of the Sea! Rule Atlantis in style with this elegant seashell crown. Gather your favourite shells together and choose the most regal-looking scallops to adorn your brow.

Materials:

- Piece of thick card – 1.5 mm thick, approx. 70 x 5.5 cm (27 x 2 in.)
- 11 cm (4 in.) piece of elastic, 1 cm (½ in.) wide
- Plenty of white copy paper, torn into pieces
- White (PVA) craft glue
- Tube of two-part rapid-set epoxy glue (60–90 second setting time)
- 5 spiral-shaped (auger) shells, approx. 7 cm (2 ¾ in.) long
- 14 assorted-size scallop shells, approx. 5 cm high x 4 cm wide (2 in. high x 1 ½ in. wide) – it's worth having more shells than you need so you can fit together the ones you like
- Handful of assorted small cockle or scallop shells, approx. 1.5 cm high x 1.5 cm wide (½ in. high x ½ in. wide)
- 50 ml (2 fl. oz) tube of gold acrylic paint
- 4–6 blue fabric flowers, no bigger than approx. 6 cm (2 ½ in.) diameter
- Approx. 28–32 blue fabric flower petals – these can be snipped from a handful of fabric flowers
- Approx. 380 cream-coloured seed beads
- 5 pieces of 20 cm (8 in.) beading thread, 0.3 mm weight
- Small pot of iridescent white or blue glitter
- Small pot of silver rhinestones

Equipment:

- Tape measure
- Metre ruler
- Scissors
- Pencil
- Masking tape
- Glue gun*
- Glass jar for mixing glue
- Paintbrushes
- Cocktail sticks
- Palette for mixing glue
- Palette for paint
- Tweezers

*If little mermaids want to try this craft, they could use quick-drying/tacky white (PVA) craft glue instead of a glue gun.

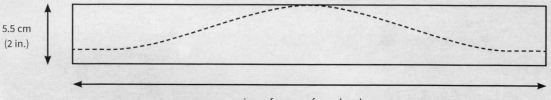

5.5 cm
(2 in.)

circumference of your head

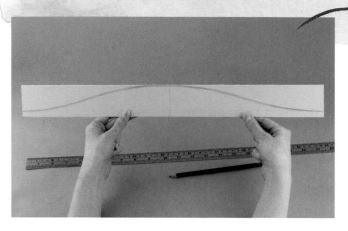

1 Start by measuring around your head with a tape measure. Cut out a headband from the thick card which is 5.5 cm (2 in.) high and the same length as the circumference of your head. Draw a wave shape onto the headband which is 1 cm (½ in.) high at both ends and slopes up to 5.5 cm (2 in.) in the middle. Cut out the headband and trim 1 cm (½ in.) off both ends (this will allow space for the elastic).

2

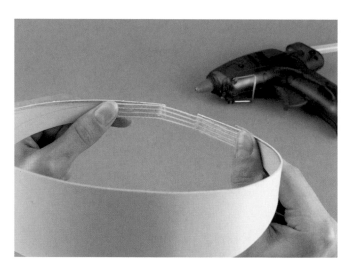

Use masking tape to temporarily stick the elastic to each (inside) end of the headband, leaving a 1 cm (½ in.) gap between the ends of the card. Carefully try on the headband and adjust the position of the elastic as necessary. When you are happy that the headband fits snuggly around your head, remove the masking tape and glue the elastic to the card with a glue gun.

3

Mix a little water with some white craft glue and papier mâché the headband with pieces of torn-up white paper, ensuring the ends of the elastic are well covered. You may want to papier mâché the headband in sections (allowing plenty of drying time between each), so that the card doesn't become too saturated with glue.

How to: papier mâché

Dip the pieces of torn-up paper into the diluted white craft glue and then paste onto the cardboard headband, overlapping the edges of the paper slightly. Smooth over the paper with your fingers or a paintbrush to flatten out any creases or bubbles.

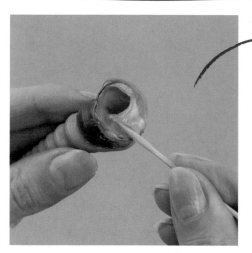

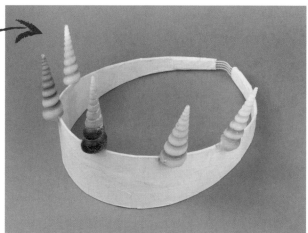

4

Mix a small amount of the two-part epoxy glue (according to the packet instructions) and use a cocktail stick to dab glue onto the end of one spiral shell. Place the shell in the middle of the headband and hold in place until the glue has dried. Glue four more spiral shells to the headband (two on either side of the central shell), leaving enough space between each for a scallop shell.

Paint the spiral shells, and the top and bottom edge of the headband in a layer of gold acrylic paint. Depending on the thickness of the paint, you may need to cover the shells in a second coat to achieve a solid colour. If so, make sure the first layer of paint is completely dry before applying the second coat.

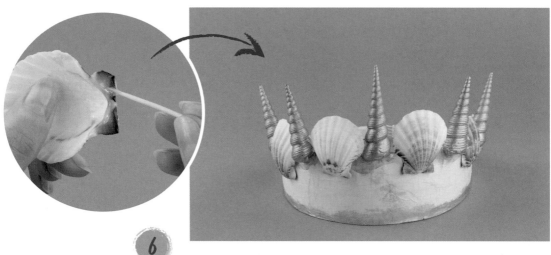

6

Mix another small amount of the two-part glue and use a cocktail stick to apply the glue to the bottom-inside edge of six scallop shells. Stick the scallop shells between each spiral shell, leaving approximately 3 cm (1 ¼ in.) of each shell overhanging the edge of the hairband. Use pieces of masking tape to hold the shells in place until the glue has dried.

 7 Overlap the first layer of scallop shells with five more scallop shells. This step is a bit like doing a jigsaw puzzle: you will need to choose shells which fit best.

 8

Glue a final layer of three scallop shells to the front of the crown, ensuring that the base of the shells meet the bottom edge of the headband. Fill any gaps at the front of the crown with small cockle or scallop shells.

 9

To cover the remaining gaps where there are no shells, stick a few fabric flowers to both sides of the headband with more epoxy glue.

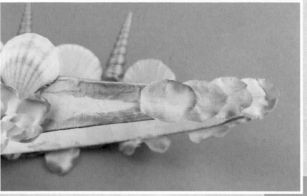

Use a glue gun to apply 14–16 flower petals to both sides of the crown. Start at the ends of the band (closest to the elastic) and overlap each petal over the last to create the impression of scales.

11

Tie a small knot in each of the five pieces of beading thread, 2–3 cm (¾–1 ¼ in.) from the ends. Thread approximately 70–80 seed beads onto each piece of thread, but don't knot the other ends of the threads yet (handle the threads carefully so that the beads do not slip off).

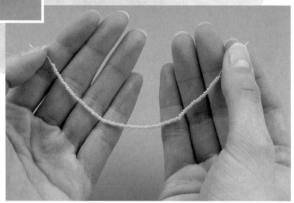

12

Temporarily stick the five threads you have beaded to the back of the crown with masking tape. Overlap two strands on each side of the crown and one across the centre. Carefully try on the crown to check that the threads hang down across your forehead but not over your eyes; according to the size of your forehead, you may need to adjust how many beads are on the threads. When you are happy with the quantity of beads and the position of the threads, knot the other ends of the threads to prevent the beads from slipping off.

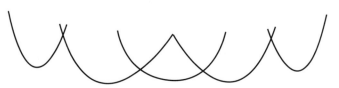

Mermaid Tip:
Why not try different shapes and sizes of seashell, or adorn your crown with interesting pieces of driftwood coated with gold or silver paint?

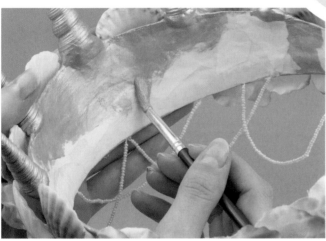

13

Remove any remaining masking tape, then papier mâché the ends of the threads to the back of the crown with more torn-up white paper (this is best done one strand at a time, allowing plenty of drying time between each). When the papier mâché is dry, paint the inside of the crown with gold acrylic paint.

14

Finally, add some sparkle to the front of your crown with rhinestones and glitter. Mix a small amount of epoxy glue and use a cocktail stick to spread a fine layer of glue over the areas you want to cover with glitter or rhinestones. Sprinkle the glitter over the glue and then shake the crown gently to dust off any excess. You may find it easier to apply rhinestones with a pair of tweezers.

Seashell Earrings

Hear the ocean wherever you go with these elegant little seashells! Perfect as a gift for one of your human friends, these dainty earrings will add a touch of seaside charm to any outfit.

Materials:

- 2 small cockle shells, approx. 1–2 cm (½–¾ in.) diameter
- 2 silver ball head pins, 5 cm (2 in.) long (plus a few extra for practice)
- 2 silver hook-shaped earring findings
- 4 small pearlescent blue beads, no bigger than 3 mm diameter
- 2 silver jump rings, 5 mm diameter

Equipment:

- 0.7–1 mm hand drill
- Plasticine (optional)
- Cutting pliers
- Flat-nosed pliers
- Round-nosed pliers

Mermaid Tip:

If you haven't made any jewellery before, you may want to practise using jewellery pliers to make loops on a few spare ball head pins or some scrap wire first.

Use a hand drill to make a small hole in the base of both cockle shells, twisting gently so that the shells do not crack. You may find it helpful to press the shells into a piece of plasticine to prevent them from slipping against your work surface.

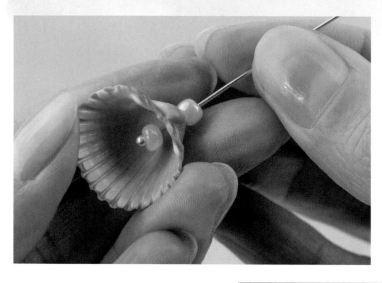

2

Thread the stem of one ball head pin through the hole in one pearlescent blue bead and through the hole in one of the cockle shells. Thread one more blue bead onto the head pin, so that the shell hangs between the two beads.

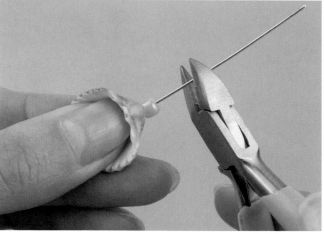

3

Push the ball of the head pin firmly up inside the shell with your thumb to prevent it from slipping. Trim off the excess stem with a pair of cutting pliers, leaving approximately 1 cm (½ in.) remaining.

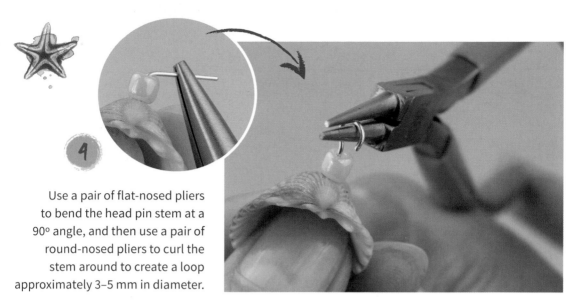

4

Use a pair of flat-nosed pliers to bend the head pin stem at a 90° angle, and then use a pair of round-nosed pliers to curl the stem around to create a loop approximately 3–5 mm in diameter.

5

Use the flat-nosed pliers to open up one jump ring, twisting ends away from one another to make a narrow gap.

6

Thread the loop of the head pin onto the jump ring, followed by one earring finding. Before you close-up the jump ring, check that the outside of the shell hangs in line with the front of the earring finding. Use the flat-nosed pliers to twist the ends of the jump ring back together.

7

Repeat Steps 2–6 for the second shell.

Fishtail Flares

Show a glimpse of your hidden mermaid tail with these shimmering fishtail flares! You could upcycle a pair of old jeans in need of some ocean magic, or transform your whole denim collection into a glimmering array of stylish fins.

Materials:

- Dark blue bootcut denim jeans, light–medium weight
- 100 x 100 cm (39 x 39 in.) piece of shimmery blue fish-scale fabric, light–medium weight
- Dark blue cotton

Equipment:

- White chalk
- Metre ruler
- Stitch unpicker
- Needles
- Fabric scissors
- Pins or iron-on fabric bond
- Iron and ironing board
- Sewing machine (suitable for medium–heavy fabrics)

Mermaid Tip:

Look for bootcut jeans which fit tightly down to the knee before they flare out slightly around the lower leg as these will give you the best flare shape.

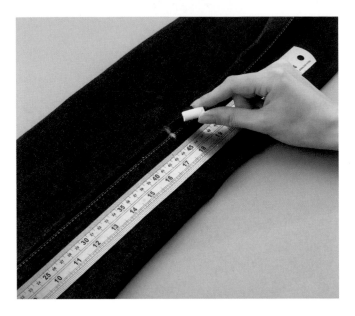

1

Use a piece of white chalk to make a small mark on the outer seams of the jeans where the bootcut shape starts to flare from the knees. Try on the jeans to check the chalk marks are in the same place on both legs. (In this example, the marks are 45 cm (18 in.) from the bottom of the jeans, but you would likely need to adjust this measurement according to your leg length.) Make a note of the measurement you have used, as you will need this later.

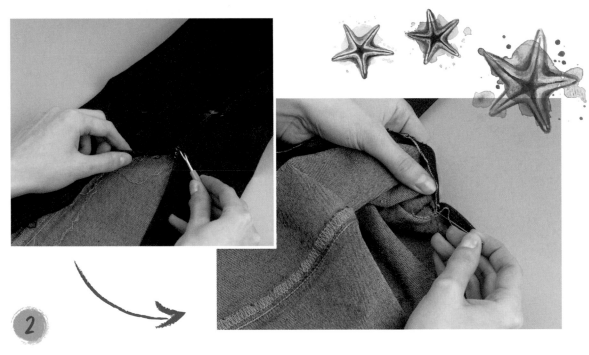

2

To open out the outer seams, snip the stitching holding the hems at the bottom of each leg (don't worry, the hems will be re-sewn later) and use a stitch unpicker to unpick both seams up to the chalk marks. Thread a small needle with dark blue cotton and sew over the loose threading at the chalk marks as this will prevent the rest of the seams unravelling.

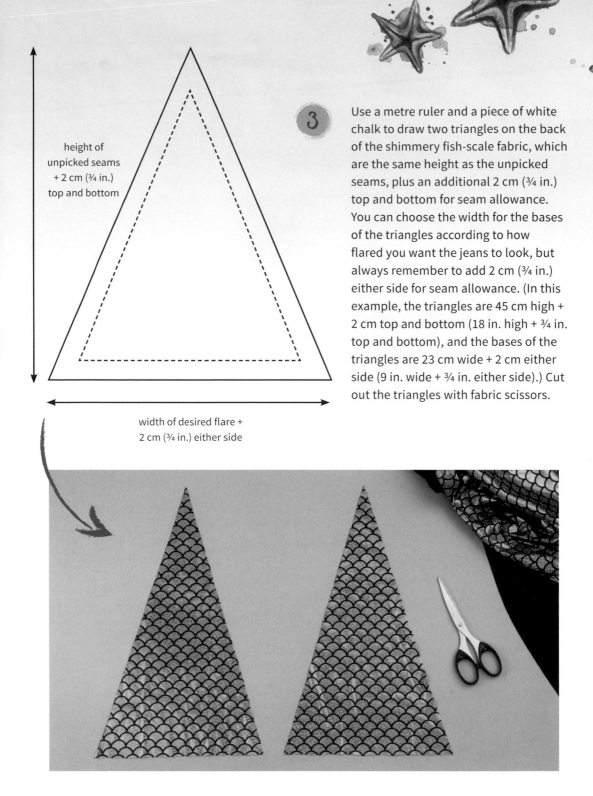

height of
unpicked seams
+ 2 cm (¾ in.)
top and bottom

width of desired flare +
2 cm (¾ in.) either side

3 Use a metre ruler and a piece of white chalk to draw two triangles on the back of the shimmery fish-scale fabric, which are the same height as the unpicked seams, plus an additional 2 cm (¾ in.) top and bottom for seam allowance. You can choose the width for the bases of the triangles according to how flared you want the jeans to look, but always remember to add 2 cm (¾ in.) either side for seam allowance. (In this example, the triangles are 45 cm high + 2 cm top and bottom (18 in. high + ¾ in. top and bottom), and the bases of the triangles are 23 cm wide + 2 cm either side (9 in. wide + ¾ in. either side).) Cut out the triangles with fabric scissors.

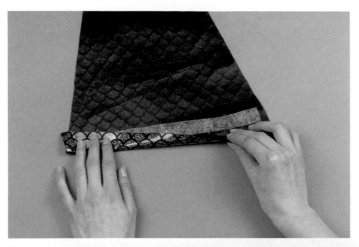

Fold up the bottom 2 cm (¾ in.) of both shimmery triangles and secure with pins or narrow pieces of iron-on fabric bond. (If you are using fabric with a particularly slippery texture, the iron-on fabric bond may be an easier option.)

Pin (or stick with iron-on fabric bond) the shimmery triangles within the open seams of the jeans, ensuring the 2 cm (¾ in.) of seam allowance at the top and sides of the triangles is hidden under the edges of the denim.

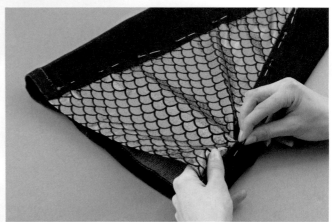

Use a sewing machine threaded with dark blue cotton to stitch the triangles into the jeans with a simple straight stitch. Starting at the bottom of the flares, stitch up the sides of each triangle, keeping the needle approximately half a centimetre away from the edge of the denim. If you are not confident using a sewing machine, you could stitch the jeans by hand with a neat backstitch.

Mermaid Tip:
If you are using a sewing machine, practise stitching a spare piece of denim and shimmery fabric to check the size and tension of your stitches are suitable for the weight of both fabrics.

 7

Re-sew the hem along the bottom of both legs with more dark blue cotton. If you are using a sewing machine, you may need to adjust the tension of the thread slightly as you move from the denim to the shimmery fabric.

 8

Finally, unpick the remnants of the old hems with a stitch unpicker.

Beachcomber Necklace

Why not turn your favourite ocean treasures into a delicate strand of seaside trinkets? Hang these pretty charms around your neck for good fortune, or give them to a mermaid friend as a good luck token for their travels across uncharted lagoons.

Materials:

For the necklace:

* Approx. 186 assorted glass or plastic beads (blue, green, pink and purple), no bigger than 5 mm diameter
* 100g ball of cream crochet yarn, thread weight
* Clear nail polish or white (PVA) craft glue
* 6 silver clamshell bead tips
* Silver screw clasp

Equipment:

* 2 mm crochet hook
* 0.7–1 mm hand drill
* Plasticine (optional)
* Flat-nosed pliers
* Round-nosed pliers
* Cutting pliers

For the pendants:

* Small scallop shell, approx. 3.5 cm high x 3 cm wide (1 ½ in. high x 1 ¼ in. wide)
* Small scallop shell, approx. 5 cm high x 4 cm wide (2 in. high x 1 ½ in. wide)
* Silver eye pin, 5 cm (2 in.) long (plus a few extra for practice)
* 6 silver jump rings, 6 mm diameter
* 3 silver jump rings, 4 mm diameter
* Piece of sea glass, approx. 3–4 cm (1 ¼–1 ½ in.) long
* 3 glass or plastic beads (blue, green, pink and purple), no bigger than 3 mm
* Pink shell chip (these are often sold with ready-made holes), approx. 3 cm (1 ¼ in.) long
* Mother of pearl disc (these are often sold with ready-made holes), approx. 1 cm (½ in.) diameter
* 15 cm (6 in.) piece of silver wire, 2 mm weight
* Tube of two-part rapid-set epoxy glue (60–90 second setting time)

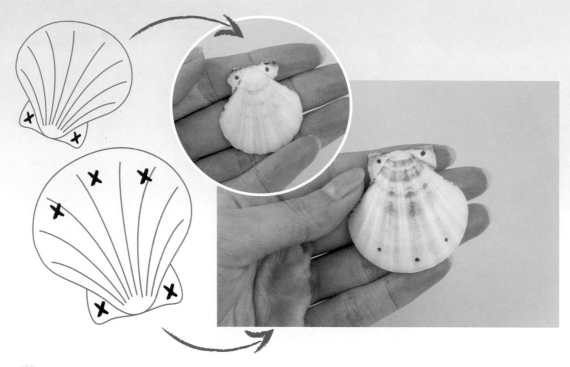

Use a hand drill to make two small holes in the wings of both scallop shells, twisting gently so that the shells do not crack. Make a further three holes along the edge of the larger shell, approximately 1 cm (½ in.) away from one another and 3 mm away from the edge of the shell. You may find it helpful to press the shells into a piece of plasticine to prevent them from slipping against your work surface.

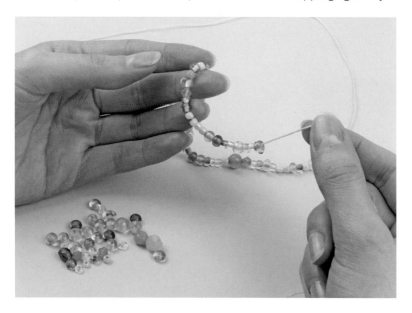

Thread approximately 53 beads onto the end of the crochet yarn (there is no need to trim the yarn off the ball). If necessary, dab a little clear nail polish or white craft glue onto the end of the yarn as this will make it easier to thread through the holes in the beads.

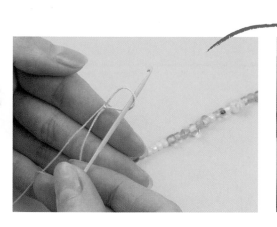

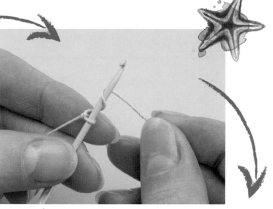

3 Loop the yarn around the stem of the crochet hook and secure with a knot, approximately 8–10 cm (3–4 in.) from the end. Pull the yarn so that the loop tightens around the stem. Wrap the yarn once around the stem and then pull the crochet hook down, catching the wrapped yarn on the hook; this will form the first stitch of the strand.

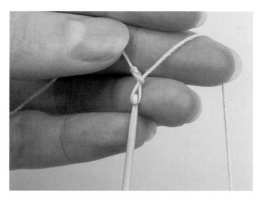

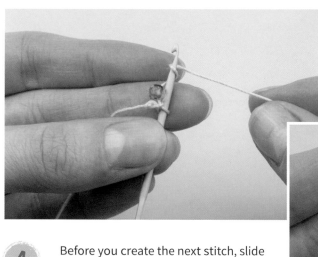

4 Before you create the next stitch, slide one bead up to the stem of the crochet hook and then wrap the yarn around the stem as you did with the previous stitch. Pull the hook down, catching the wrapped yarn on the hook as you go.

If you haven't crocheted anything before, you may want to practise on a few spare threads of yarn. Crocheting with beads can be fiddly, but once you develop a steady rhythm, you'll find it's quite easy.

5 Continue alternating between non-beaded stitches and beaded stitches, until you have used up all the beads on the yarn. Cut the beaded strand free from the ball, leaving 8–10 cm (2–5 in.) of spare yarn at the end. Gently remove the crochet hook from the strand and pass the end of the yarn through the last stitch. Tie a knot in the strand to prevent it from unravelling, but do not trim off the excess yarn.

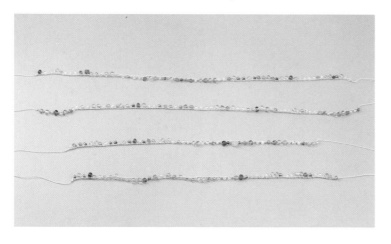

6 Repeat Steps 2–5 to create a second strand of approximately 53 beads, then repeat twice more but create two shorter strands using approximately 40 beads on each. You should now have two long strands and two short strands of beaded crochet.

7

Thread the end of one long strand and one short strand together through the hole in one clamshell bead tip. Tie the ends together in a knot and trim off the excess yarn with a pair of scissors. Fix the knot with a little clear nail polish or white craft glue and then press the two halves of the clamshell together with a pair of flat-nosed pliers. Repeat this step for the other long and short strands.

8

Use the flat-nosed pliers to open up the loops on both sides of the screw clasp with a slight twisting motion. Thread the clamshell bead tips at the ends of the strands onto each open loop and then use the flat-nosed pliers to twist both loops back together. You should now have one long strand and one short strand attached to both sides of the screw clasp.

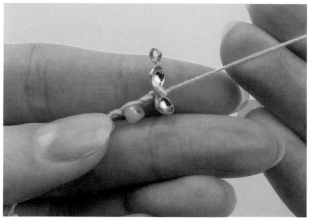

9

Thread the remaining four ends of the beaded strands through the holes in four more clamshell bead tips. Tie a small knot in each thread and trim off the excess. Fix the knots with a small dab of clear nail polish or white craft glue and then close up the clamshells with the flat-nosed pliers.

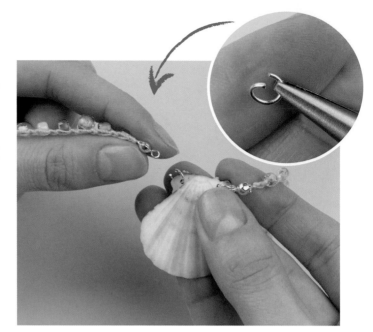

10

Use the flat-nosed pliers to open up two 4 mm jump rings, twisting the ends away from one another to make a narrow gap. Thread the open jump rings through the holes in the wings of the small scallop shell. Thread the clamshells, at the ends of the short beaded strands, onto the open jump rings and then twist the ends of the rings back together with the flat-nosed pliers.

11

Open up two 6 mm jump rings with the flat-nosed pliers and thread the open rings through the holes in the wings of the larger scallop shell. Thread the clamshell bead tips at the ends of the two long strands onto the open jump rings and then twist the ends of the rings back together. You should now have a double-stranded necklace with two shell pendants.

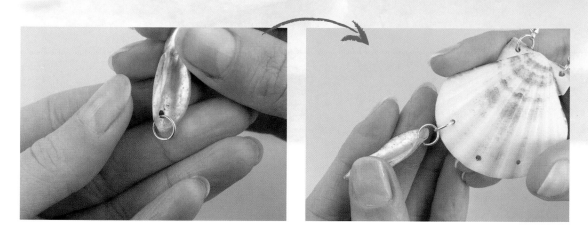

12 Twist open two more 6 mm jump rings with the flat-nosed pliers. Thread one jump ring through the hole in the pink shell chip and then twist the ends back together. Thread the other jump ring through the hole on the left side of the larger scallop shell and then through the jump ring on the shell chip. Twist the ends back together with the flat-nosed pliers.

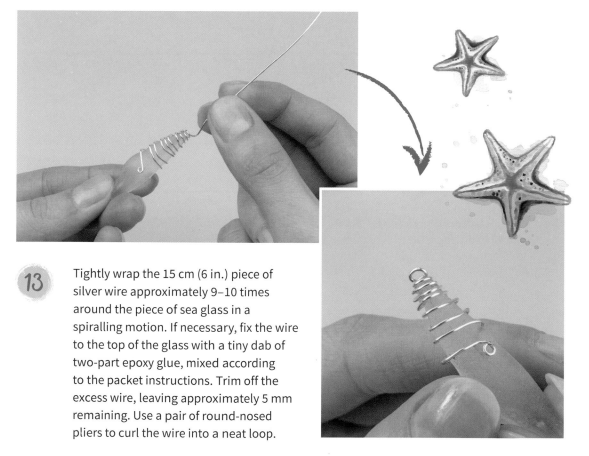

13 Tightly wrap the 15 cm (6 in.) piece of silver wire approximately 9–10 times around the piece of sea glass in a spiralling motion. If necessary, fix the wire to the top of the glass with a tiny dab of two-part epoxy glue, mixed according to the packet instructions. Trim off the excess wire, leaving approximately 5 mm remaining. Use a pair of round-nosed pliers to curl the wire into a neat loop.

14

Use the flat-nosed pliers to open up one 6 mm jump ring. Thread the jump ring through the middle hole in the edge of the large scallop shell and then through the loop you created at the top of the sea glass. Twist the ends of the jump ring back together.

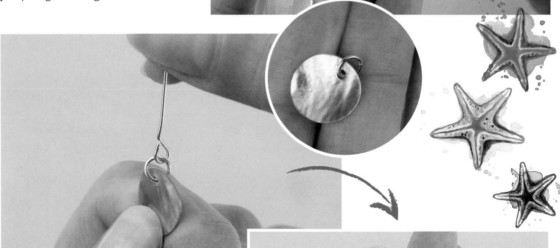

15

Open up one 4 mm jump ring and thread through the hole in the mother of pearl disc and then through the hole in the eye pin. Slide three beads onto the eye pin and then bend the stem at a 90° angle using the flat-nosed pliers. Trim off the excess stem, leaving approximately 5 mm remaining.

16 Use the round-nosed pliers to curl the remaining 5 mm piece of stem into a neat loop. (You may want to practise making loops on a few spare eye pins first.) Twist open one more 6 mm jump ring and thread through the final hole in the large scallop shell and through the loop you created in the eye pin. Close up the jump ring with the flat-nosed pliers.

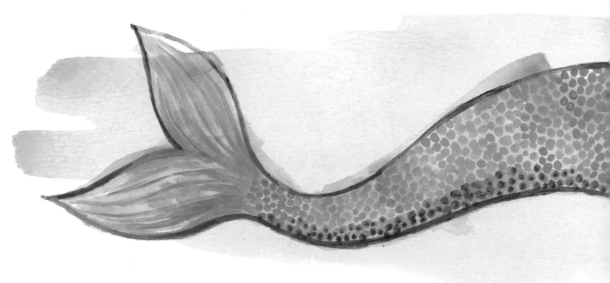

Boho Beach Flip-Flops

If you really have to walk on land, make a splash with these stylish boho flip-flops. If you do swap your fins for feet, you're sure to step out of the waves in style! Why not upcycle a pair of old flip-flops for a fresh, summery look?

Materials:

- Plain coloured flip-flops with faux leather or fabric straps
- Roll of "vintage" cream lace, wide enough to cover the flip-flop straps
- 2 pink-tinged scallop shells, approx. 5 cm high x 4 cm wide (2 in. high x 1 ½ in. wide)
- 6 pearl beads, no bigger than 3 mm diameter
- Cream cotton thread
- 6 pieces of 20 cm (8 in.) cream crochet yarn, thread weight
- Approx. 60–70 pink shimmery beads, no bigger than 3 mm diameter
- White (PVA) craft glue

Equipment:

- Tape measure
- Scissors
- Pins
- Sewing needles
- Thimble (optional)
- Pencil
- 0.7–1 mm hand drill
- Plasticine (optional)
- Fabric glue

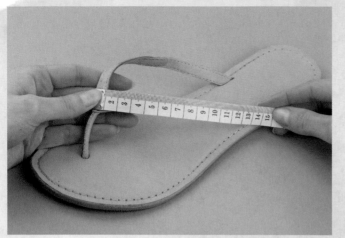

1

Measure both straps of one flip-flop with a tape measure and cut two pieces of lace slightly longer than these measurements. (The strap on the outer side of the flip-flop will likely be slightly longer than the inner strap.)

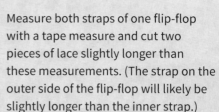

2

Pin the pieces of lace securely to the flip-flop straps and trim off any excess with a pair of scissors so that the edges of the lace fit snuggly against the sole of the flip-flop.

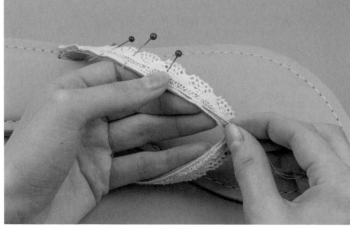

3

Thread a small needle with the cream-coloured cotton and sew the pieces of lace to the flip-flop with a simple backstitch. (Faux leather can be a little tough to stitch through, so you may want to use a thimble to protect your fingers.)

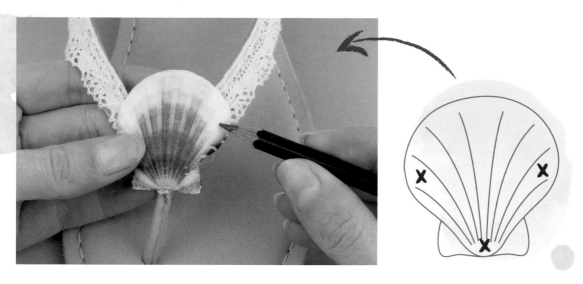

 Position one scallop shell over the front of the flip-flop and make three small pencil marks on the surface of the shell: one at the base and two either side. Make sure the pencil marks line up with the middle of the straps beneath, and are at least 3 mm away from the edges of the shell.

 Use a hand drill to make three neat holes where you made the pencil marks. Don't apply too much pressure as you twist the drill or you may crack the shell. You may find it helpful to press the shell into a piece of plasticine to prevent it from slipping against your work surface.

Mermaid Tip:

Because this craft will be unique to your foot size, it is a good idea to measure your flip-flops before you go shopping for craft materials. If in doubt, buy more materials than you think you will need; the leftover bits and bobs can always be used for other crafts (see pages 95 or 146).

6

Thread a sharp needle with one piece of crochet yarn. Push the needle up through the point where the flip-flop straps meet (just above the toe post) and then up through the hole in the base of the scallop shell.

7

Thread one pearl bead onto the crochet yarn, and then pass the needle back through the hole in the shell and back through the flip-flop strap.

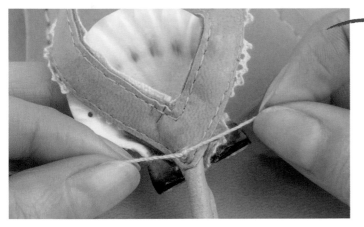

8 Tie the ends of the crochet yarn in a small, tight knot on the underside of the straps. Fix the knots with a small dab of white craft glue and then trim off the excess yarn. Repeat Steps 6–7 for the other two holes in the shell.

9

Thread a small needle with the cream-coloured cotton and sew a row of approximately 15 shimmery pink beads along the edge of each strap. Depending on the size of your flip-flops, you may need to adjust this quantity.

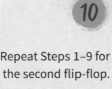

10 Repeat Steps 1–9 for the second flip-flop.

Splattered Scales Tote Bag

Save the ocean and shop in style with this reusable tote bag on your shoulder. All your mermaid friends will be asking where you found this gorgeous, colourful bag!

Materials:

- Lightweight white cotton tote bag, approx. 42 cm high x 36 cm wide (16 in. high x 14 in. wide)
- 300 g (10 ½ oz) white wax flakes
- 25 ml (1 fl. oz) pot of pink "stay soft" fabric paint
- 25 ml (1 fl. oz) pot of purple "stay soft" fabric paint
- 25 ml (1 fl. oz) pot of turquoise "stay soft" fabric paint
- White card (1 mm thick), trimmed to fit inside the tote bag
- Scrap card (2 mm thick), trimmed to fit inside the tote bag

Equipment:

- Waterproof black pen
- Chopping board
- Knife
- Heatproof jug
- Microwave
- Spoon
- Paintbrushes
- 3 glass jars
- Paper towels (you could use kitchen roll)
- Iron and ironing board

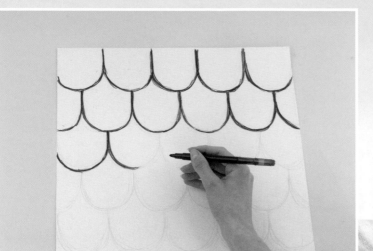

1

Use a waterproof black pen to draw a fish-scale pattern onto the white card; you should be able to fit approximately five scales across and six scales down. You could enlarge the template on page 156.

2

Iron the tote bag to remove any creases and then slip the fish-scale pattern inside (the black lines should be visible through the fabric). Place the wax flakes in a heat-proof jug and melt in the microwave using 30 second bursts, stirring with a metal spoon between each heating.

3

Use a medium-sized paintbrush to paint the melted wax onto the bag, following the fish-scale pattern as a guide. Make sure each brushstroke transfers enough wax to really soak into the fibres of the fabric. When the wax has hardened, remove the card with the pattern from within the bag and set it aside to be used again later for the reverse.

Pour a small quantity of each fabric paint into separate glass jars. Mix the paints with a little water, until they drip easily from a brush (the more water you add, the paler the dried paint will be).

Before painting the bag, slip the piece of thick card inside the tote to prevent the colour from soaking through to the other side.

Splatter the three colours of diluted paint across the tote bag with a large brush; the wax will repel the paint and reveal your fish-scale design.

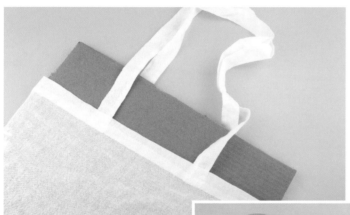

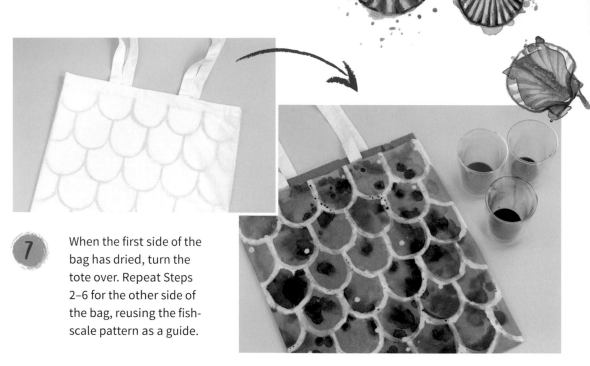

7 When the first side of the bag has dried, turn the tote over. Repeat Steps 2–6 for the other side of the bag, reusing the fish-scale pattern as a guide.

8

Paint both sides of the bag straps with more diluted fabric paint.

Mermaid Tip:

This can get very messy, so make sure you have plenty of scrap newspaper or a plastic sheet to protect your work surface and wear an apron to protect your clothes!

9

When the paint is completely dry, scrunch the bag in your hands to flake off the wax. The more wax you can remove in this way, the better.

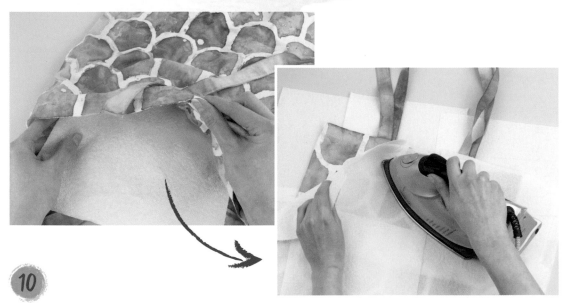

10

To remove the rest of the wax, line the inside and outside of the tote with plenty of paper towels and iron on a low heat to melt the wax into the paper. Remove the towels from both the inside and outside of the bag before the wax re-solidifies and, if necessary, repeat this process again. To fix the fabric paint, cover the bag in a fresh layer of paper towels and iron on a medium heat. (Most fabric paints require ironing on a medium–high heat to fix the colour, but always check the instructions for your chosen brand.)

Mermaid Bra

Bored of your usual clam shells? Well, don't get disheartened if your wardrobe is looking a little dull, you're sure to sparkle and shine again in this pretty peppermint bra!

Materials:

- Blue cotton thread
- Approx. 150–170 blue satin petals, 2 cm (¾ in.) diameter (these can be snipped from a handful of silk flowers)
- Peppermint green bra (underwired and padded)
- Paper (optional)
- Roll of ready-strung iridescent pink or white sequins
- Small bag of turquoise seed beads (approx. 260–280)
- Small bag of pale blue seed beads (approx. 240–260)
- 6 large turquoise fabric petals
- Roll of sparkly frill-edged peppermint green ribbon
- Roll of ready-strung beaded thread
- 20–24 navette-shaped sew-on rhinestones, approx. 15 mm long x 7 mm wide
- 20–30 circular sew-on rhinestones, approx. 4 mm diameter

Equipment:

- Pencil
- Tape measure
- Scissors
- Sewing needles
- Mirror

Mermaid Tip:

Because this craft will be unique to your body size, it is a good idea to measure your bra before you go shopping for craft materials. If in doubt, buy more materials than you think you will need; the leftover bits and bobs can always be used for other crafts (see pages 95 or 146).

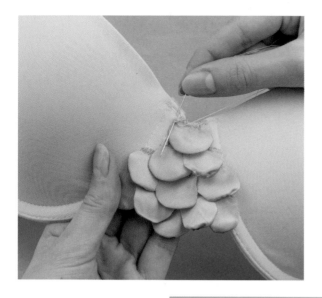

Thread a small needle with blue cotton and sew 4–5 rows of satin petals to the centre bridge of the bra (between the cups). Starting at the bottom of the bridge, overlay each row of petals to hide your stitching on the previous row. You should be able to fit between 10–13 petals here, depending on the size of your bra, but you may need to adjust this quantity slightly. Sew more overlapping rows of petals to both sides of the bra, until the bands on either side are completely hidden.

Use a pencil to lightly sketch three rounded petal shapes across the front of both cups. (If you aren't confident sketching directly onto the bra, you could practise your design on paper first.)

Starting from the inner edges of each cup, sew the ready-threaded sequins over the petal shapes with pale blue cotton, hiding your stitches under the sequins. Don't worry about pre-cutting lengths of sequins, just trim them off the roll as you reach the end of each petal.

4

Stitch sparkly green ribbon over the underwired areas of the bra with a discreet back stitch, starting from the inner edge of each cup. Cut the ribbon off the roll once you reach the other end of each underwire and sew over the raw edges to prevent them from fraying.

5

Sew a fan-shaped cluster of rhinestones to the inner area of both cups. In this example, approximately 10–12 navette-shaped rhinestones were used on each side of the bra, but you may need to adjust this quantity according to the size of your cups. Scatter 10–15 small circular rhinestones around the edges of the fan shape.

6 Sew a single turquoise seed bead to the middle of each sequin, passing the needle up through the hole in the sequin, though the hole in a seed bead and back down through the sequin again.

7 Decorate the outer edges of each cup (outside the sequin petals) with clusters of pale blue seed beads, spaced a few millimetres apart.

8 Sew three large turquoise petals to the top of each cup where the strap joins onto the padded material. Cover your stitches with 3–5 navette-shaped rhinestones and a cluster of pale blue seed beads.

Mermaid Tip:

Good news: your bra is washable! Always wash gently by hand in cool water to avoid dislodging any beads.

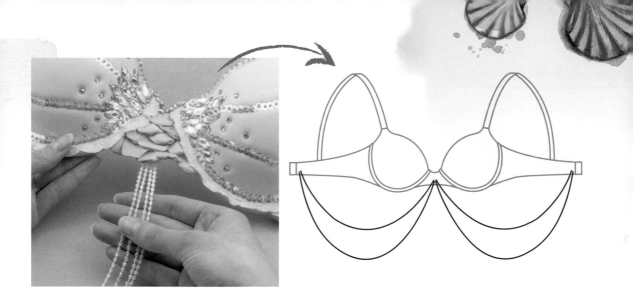

9 Stand in front of a mirror (or ask a mermaid friend to help!) and cut four pieces of ready-strung beaded thread which hang either side of your body, from the front of the bra to the clasp at the back. Sew all four pieces to the back of the bridge (underneath the layered scales), placing the shortest pieces on the outside. Gather the ends of one short and one long piece together and stitch to the end of one side band (close to the bra hooks), hiding your stitches under the layered petals. Gather the other long and short pieces together and stitch to the end of the other side band. The pieces of beaded thread should hang down from the front of your bra, across your ribs and back up and around to the back of your bra.

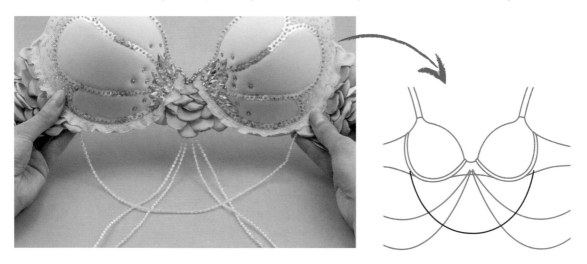

10 Trim one more piece of ready-strung beaded thread which will hang in a loop between the cups of the bra. Tuck the ends of the thread underneath the first layer of satin petals, next to the underwires on either side of the cups. Stitch in place with more blue cotton.

Sea Glass Ring

Materials:

- Adjustable silver ring blank
- Piece of pretty sea glass, approx. 1–1.5 cm (½–¾ in.) diameter*
- Tube of two-part rapid-set epoxy glue (60–90 second setting time)

You drift through the shallows, sifting through the sand and the sea-smoothed pebbles for a perfect piece of sea glass. With this unique ring, you'll be able to carry a little piece of the beach wherever you go.

*If little mermaids want to try this craft, they could use a frosted plastic bead as this will be safer than using a piece of glass.

Equipment:

- Fine-grain sandpaper
- Palette for mixing glue
- Cocktail stick

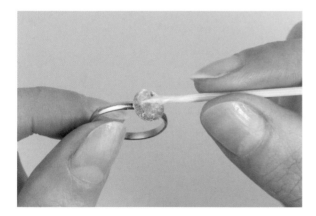

1 Scuff the surface of the ring plate with the sandpaper. Then mix a small amount of two-part epoxy glue (according to the packet instructions) and use a cocktail stick to spread the glue onto the plate.

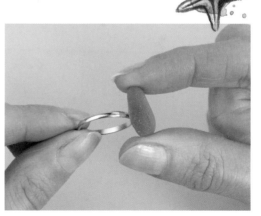

2 Press the sea glass onto the plate and hold it in place until the glue has set.

Beach Beauty

*Magical mermaid
hair and make-up!*

Mer-mazing Make-up

Your invite has arrived for the annual Atlantean ball! With this dazzling make-up, you can transform even your simplest outfit into a mesmerizing new look.

Materials:

- Liquid or mousse foundation, to match your skin tone (optional)
- Translucent powder, to match your skin tone (optional)
- Highlighting powder (optional)
- Bronzing powder (optional)
- Blue eyeshadow
- Purple eyeshadow
- Pink eyeshadow
- Black eyeliner pencil
- Black mascara
- Make-up fixing spray
- Petroleum jelly
- Small pot of iridescent blue biodegradable body glitter
- Silver sticky-back rhinestones
- Pink shimmery lip gloss

Equipment:

- Make-up brush set
- Fishnet tights

Mermaid Tip:

Before you begin, make sure your face is freshly washed and lightly moisturized; foundation will blend better if your skin is well hydrated. If you don't want to use foundation, you can skip the first step.

1 Apply an even layer of foundation to your face in your preferred way, then use a large make-up brush to "fix" the foundation with a light dusting of translucent powder. Sweep highlighter over the top of your cheekbones, brow arch and cupid's bow, and accent the lower edge of your cheekbones with a little bronzer.

2 Dab a generous amount of blue eyeshadow over your eyelids and around your eyes with a small make-up brush.

3 Exaggerate the outer edges of your eyes with purple and/or pink eyeshadow, blending the colours together across the top of your eyelids. Use a clean brush to gently dust away any fallen powder which has settled below your eyes.

4 Line both your top and bottom outer lash line with black eyeliner and coat your lashes in black mascara. Make sure your mascara has fully dried before moving on to the next step.

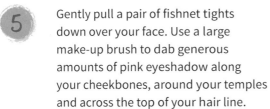

5 Gently pull a pair of fishnet tights down over your face. Use a large make-up brush to dab generous amounts of pink eyeshadow along your cheekbones, around your temples and across the top of your hair line.

6 Lift the tights carefully off your face to reveal your scales! Spritz your face with a little make-up fixer before moving on to the next step.

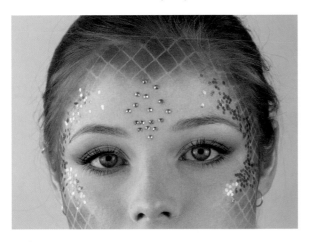

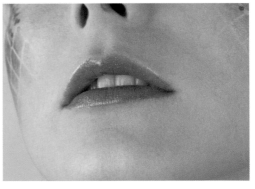

7 To add a touch of shimmer to your mermaid look, stick a cluster of small rhinestones in the middle of your forehead. Use your fingertips to dab a fine layer of petroleum jelly over your cheekbones and then lightly dust glitter over the jelly.

8 Finally, coat your lips with pink shimmery lip gloss.

Ocean Wave Soap

Bring the sparkle back to your scales and the glimmer back to your fins with this gorgeous ocean soap. Not only does it look like a slice of the sea, it will smell like a tropical paradise too!

Materials:

- 700 g (1 lb 9 oz) of clear "melt and pour" soap base
- 300 g (10 ½ oz) of white "melt and pour" soap base
- 5 ml (¼ fl. oz) bottle of dark blue liquid soap dye
- 5 ml (¼ fl. oz) bottle of turquoise liquid soap dye
- 5 ml (¼ fl. oz) bottle of aqua liquid soap dye
- 5 ml (¼ fl. oz) bottle of coconut fragrance oil (or an essential oil of your choice)
- 300 ml (10 fl. oz) of 90% IPA alcohol

Equipment:

- Fine, sharp-bladed knife
- Chopping board
- 2 heat-proof jugs
- Microwave
- Metal spoon
- Rectangular silicone soap mould, 1 kg (2 lb 3 oz) capacity (example used here: 25 cm long x 6 cm wide x 7 cm deep (9 in. long x 2 ½ in. wide x 2 ¾ in. deep))
- Wooden soap box, to fit the silicone soap mould
- 2 small scallop or cockle shells
- Spray bottle (for IPA alcohol)

Cut the clear soap base into small pieces with a sharp knife and place a third of the chopped soap into a heat-proof jug (set aside the rest of the clear soap for later). Microwave the jug for a minute or two until the soap is melted; you may need to stir the soap with a spoon and return to the microwave a few times.

To create the darkest layer, gradually drip dark blue dye into the melted soap base until it turns a deep blue. It is best to do this a drop or two at a time (stirring between each), so as not to add too much colour in one go. Add a few drops of coconut fragrance oil (or a fragrance of your choice) and stir again.

Prop up one side of the soap mould with two small scallop shells; this will tilt the mould so that the soap slants diagonally.

4 Carefully pour the soap into the mould and spray the surface with IPA alcohol to remove any bubbles created during pouring.

5

When the soap has set but is still warm, push the surface gently either with your fingers or with a rounded object (like the end of a spoon), to create indentations which look like waves. (Make sure to wash your hands well before doing this, as contaminating the soap may prevent the layers from sticking together properly.)

6

Chop the white soap base into small pieces and place a third of the chopped soap into a clean heat-proof jug (set aside the rest of the white soap for later). Melt the white soap in the microwave, stirring and returning to the microwave if necessary.

7

Before you pour the white soap into the mould, spray the blue layer thoroughly with IPA alcohol; this will ensure the layers stick together. Drizzle the white soap over the blue, allowing it to pool in the indentations. Once poured, spray again with IPA alcohol to remove any bubbles.

8

Reuse the first measuring jug to melt another third of the clear soap base. This time, add turquoise dye to create the next shade. Again, it is best to do this a few drops at a time so that you don't add too much colour at once. Add a few drops of coconut fragrance and stir again.

Mermaid Tip:

The key to good soap making is to remember to spray the soap with IPA alcohol before and after you pour each layer. If you forget this step, the soap layers may not bond together and could split apart when cut.

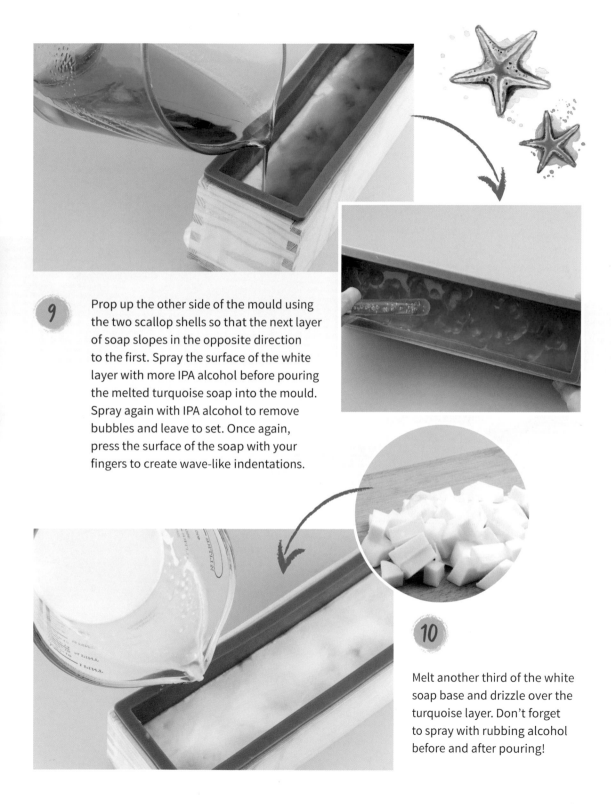

9 Prop up the other side of the mould using the two scallop shells so that the next layer of soap slopes in the opposite direction to the first. Spray the surface of the white layer with more IPA alcohol before pouring the melted turquoise soap into the mould. Spray again with IPA alcohol to remove bubbles and leave to set. Once again, press the surface of the soap with your fingers to create wave-like indentations.

10 Melt another third of the white soap base and drizzle over the turquoise layer. Don't forget to spray with rubbing alcohol before and after pouring!

11 Melt the final third of clear soap, this time adding a just a couple of drops of aqua dye to create the palest shade. Add a few drops of coconut fragrance and stir again. Once again, tilt the mould in the opposite direction. Spray the surface of the soap with IPA alcohol before pouring the final layer of coloured soap. Spray again to remove any bubbles created when pouring. When the soap has partially set, press the surface to create more indentations.

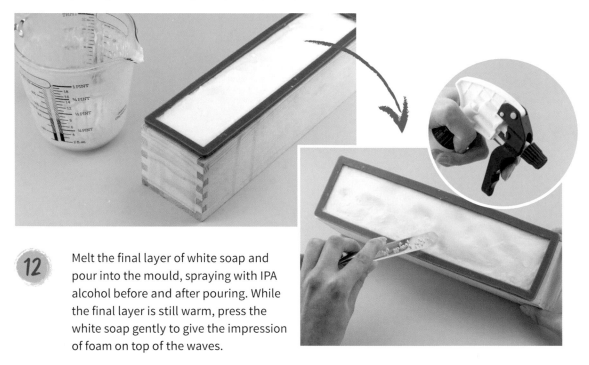

12 Melt the final layer of white soap and pour into the mould, spraying with IPA alcohol before and after pouring. While the final layer is still warm, press the white soap gently to give the impression of foam on top of the waves.

If you are not going to use your finished soap bars immediately, wrap them up in waxed paper and place in a sealed container. Some soap bases contain ingredients which will attract water from the air, which can make it look as if the soap is oozing beads of liquid. This won't harm your soap, but it won't make it look very pretty!

 13 When the last layer of soap has fully hardened, slide the silicone mould out of its supporting wooden box. Peel the silicone mould gently off the soap to reveal your ocean waves!

 14

Lay the soap block on its side and use a fine, sharp-bladed knife to slice the soap into five or six bars. It is best to cut the soap within a few hours after the last layer has set; if you leave the soap for too long it will harden and become difficult to cut.

Pretty Pearl Pins

Let the ocean spray wash these pretty pearls into your hair as you swim in the shallows! These simple pins are perfect for adding a sprinkle of shimmer to a simple braid, or as the finishing touch to an elegant up-do.

Materials:

- 5–10 hair pins, to match your hair colour
- 5–10 pieces of 15 cm (6 in.) long silver wire, 0.2 mm weight
- 5–10 pearl beads, assorted sizes and colours

Equipment:

- Cutting pliers

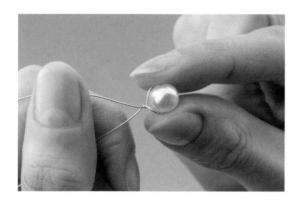

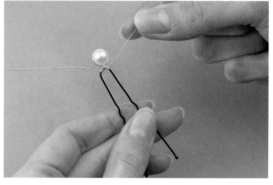

 1 Slide one pearl bead onto the middle of one piece of wire. Fold the ends of the wire down and twist together a few times below the bead.

 2 Wrap the ends of the wire tightly around the top of each hairpin "leg"; four–five loops on each side should be enough to secure the bead in place.

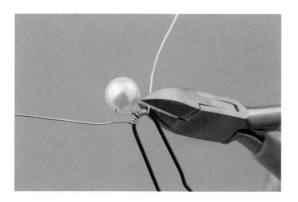

 3 Trim off the excess wire with a pair of cutting pliers. Repeat Steps 1–3 for the other pins.

Fish-Scale Nails

Why not treat yourself and some of your mermaid friends to a stylish nail makeover? You don't have to use the colours suggested here; you could match the colour of your nails to the colour of your tails.

Materials:

- 10 sticky-back fish-scale nail stencils
- 5 ml (¼ fl. oz) bottle of white nail polish
- 5 ml (¼ fl. oz) bottle of dark blue nail polish
- 5 ml (¼ fl. oz) bottle of mid-blue nail polish
- 5 ml (¼ fl. oz) bottle of peppermint green nail polish
- 5 ml (¼ fl. oz) bottle of clear nail polish
- 10 iridescent rhinestones

Equipment:

- Palette
- Small sponge
- Tweezers
- A friend to help (optional)

Memaid Tip:

You may find it helpful to practise sponging onto a plain piece of paper, or try out a "test" nail before you paint all of them.

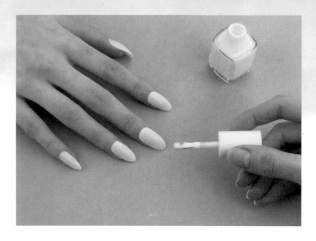

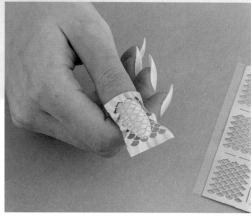

1 Before you begin, make sure your nails are clean, dry and free from existing polish. Paint each nail with one to two coats of white nail polish, allowing plenty of drying time between each coat.

2 When the white polish has completely hardened, gently stick one fish-scale stencil over one of your thumb nails. Press the stencil lightly with your fingers to make sure all the small areas are stuck to the nail. (You may want to ask a mermaid friend to help you with the following steps!)

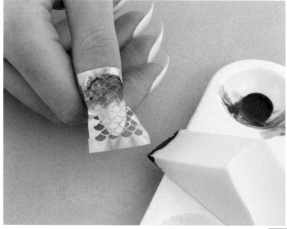

3 Pour a small amount of dark blue nail polish onto a paint palette. Dip a small sponge in the dark blue polish and dab onto a clear area of the palette to remove excess polish. Lightly sponge the dark blue polish over the bottom third of the thumb nail.

4 Use a clean area of the sponge to dab mid-blue polish over the middle of the nail, overlapping the colours slightly so that they blend together to create a gradient.

5

Repeat again with the peppermint green polish, dabbing the sponge over the remaining tip of the nail.

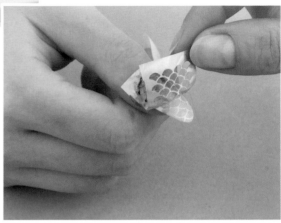

6

While the polish is still wet, gently peel the stencil off the nail to reveal your scales! Repeat Steps 2–6 for the rest of your nails, using a fresh stencil each time. When all your nails have been stencilled, leave them to harden for at least half an hour before moving on to the next step.

7
Paint each nail in a layer of clear polish. Try to avoid sweeping the brush too many times over the nails or you may start to dissolve the scales below; two confident strokes should be enough to cover an entire nail in polish.

8
While the clear nail polish is still wet, use a pair of tweezers to carefully position a single rhinestone at the base of each nail. Press the rhinestones lightly with your fingertips to help them bond to the polish. When your nails are completely dry, coat each in one final layer of clear polish.

Golden Comb

All that swimming can leave your hair in quite a mess! So, next time you stop by your favourite lagoon to admire your reflection, don't get distressed if your tresses look a bit washed-up. Use this pretty golden comb to brush away the tangles... singing is optional.

Materials:

- Wooden comb, approx. 10 cm long x 5 cm high (4 in. long x 2 in. high)

- Tube of two-part rapid-set epoxy glue (60–90 second setting time)

- Small scallop shell, approx. 5 cm high x 4 cm wide (2 in. high x 1 ½ in wide)

- 10 g (½ oz) of two-part self-hardening epoxy clay (5 g (¼ oz) of each part)

- 25 ml (1 fl. oz) tube of gold acrylic paint

- 25 ml (1 fl. oz) tube of bronze acrylic paint

- Small bottle of satin acrylic varnish

Equipment:

- Fine-grain sandpaper

- Damp cloth

- Palette for mixing glue

- Cocktail stick

- Pencil

- Paper (optional)

- Craft mat

- Paintbrushes

- Small jar of water

- Palette for paint

1

Thoroughly sand the surface of the comb with a piece of sandpaper to remove any existing varnish or paint. Wipe the comb with a damp cloth to clean off loose dust and grit.

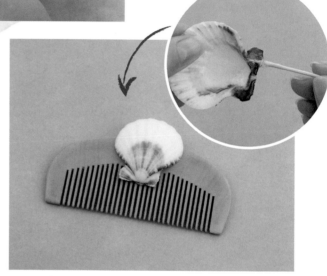

2

Mix a small amount of the two-part epoxy glue (according to the packet instructions) and use a cocktail stick to carefully spread the glue along the bottom inside edge of the scallop shell. Stick the shell to the middle of the comb, allowing the top edge to overhang by approximately 1 cm (½ in.). Hold the shell in place until the glue has set.

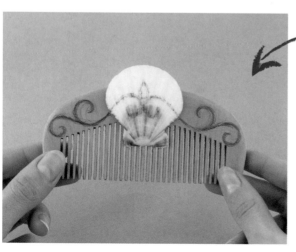

3

Lightly sketch a symmetrical swirly design onto the comb and over the top of the shell with a pencil; this can be as simple or as intricate as you like! If you are creating your own pattern, you may want to plan your design on paper first, or you could enlarge the template on page 157.

Two-part epoxy clay is self-hardening and does not need to be baked; it will harden within a few hours of mixing. Although water will smooth the surface of the clay, it will not prevent the clay from eventually setting. Often, two-part clay can be a little soft or sticky when first mixed, which can make it more difficult to sculpt. If this is the case, leave the clay for 10–15 minutes to firm-up a little before sculpting.

4

Thoroughly mix the two parts of the modelling clay (according to the packet instructions) and roll small balls of clay into string-like pieces, approximately 3 mm in diameter. Check that the pieces are long enough to cover your pencil sketch.

5 Lay the pieces of clay over the top of your sketched design and press gently to stick the clay to the surface of the comb. Use your fingertips to blend the edges of the clay onto the wood. Don't worry if the clay becomes discoloured by the pencil marks.

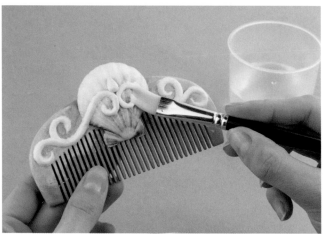

Smooth away any fingerprints on the surface of the clay with a paintbrush dipped in water and then leave in a dust-free place to harden. Most two-part clays will usually set within a few hours, but check the packet instructions for your chosen brand if you are unsure.

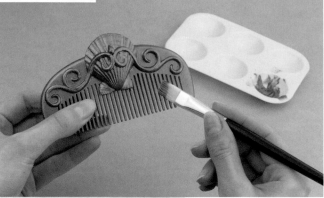

7 Paint the whole comb with an even layer of bronze acrylic paint. Depending on the thickness of the paint, you may need to cover the comb in a second coat to achieve a solid colour.

8

To create an antique, aged-metal effect, use a small paintbrush dipped in gold paint to highlight areas of detail; dab the brush on the side of your palette to remove most of the paint, and then "dry brush" the remaining paint over the scallop shell and the clay swirls.

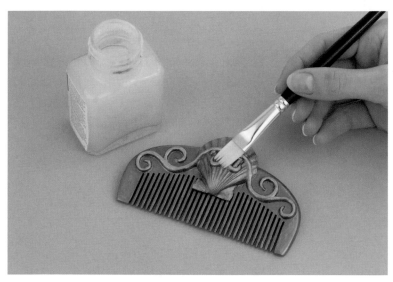

9

Finally, glaze the comb with a layer of satin acrylic varnish, allowing plenty of drying time between each side.

Sparkly Seaweed Hair

Going to a party on the reef and can't think what to do with your hair? Why not whip up this simple hairpiece to add a dash of sparkle to your locks? Simple to make and simple to wear, all your ocean friends will want to know who styled your hair!

Materials:

- Peppermint green cotton
- Clip-on peppermint green hairpiece, trimmed to your hair length
- 3–4 pieces of translucent shimmery blue ribbon, trimmed to your hair length
- 2 pieces of ready-strung iridescent beads, trimmed to your hair length
- String of ready-threaded sequins, trimmed to your hair length
- 3 pieces of peppermint green embroidery thread, trimmed to your hair length
- Clear nail polish or white (PVA) craft glue

Equipment:

- Needles
- Scissors

Mermaid Tip:

Get creative! This craft is an excellent way of using up any scrap bits of ribbon or thread you may have left over from other crafts.

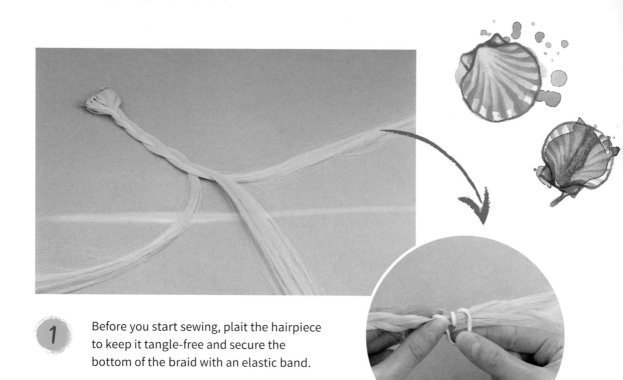

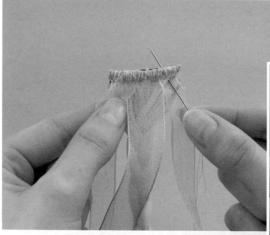

1. Before you start sewing, plait the hairpiece to keep it tangle-free and secure the bottom of the braid with an elastic band.

2. Thread a small needle with blue cotton and sew the pieces of translucent, blue ribbon side-by-side to the top of the hairpiece. When you have finished stitching, don't trim the cotton, move straight on to the next step.

3. Position the two pieces of ready-strung beads side-by-side on the right side of the hair clip. Loop a few stitches between the beads and through the hair beneath.

Hold the string of sequins in the middle of the hairpiece and fix in place with a few stitches that pass through the hole in the first sequin. Knot the thread discreetly behind the hair and trim off any excess cotton.

Tie a knot at one end of each piece of embroidery thread. Thread a medium-sized needle with one piece of embroidery thread and pass the needle up through the hairpiece, hiding the knot behind the hair. Repeat with the other two pieces of embroidery thread.

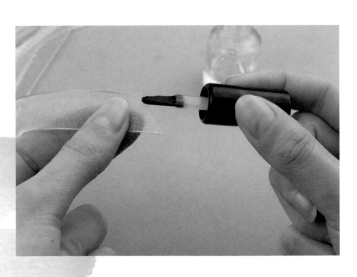

Fix any raw edges which may fray with a dab of clear nail polish or white craft glue. When dry, remove the elastic band and un-plait the hair.

Starfish Hairband

This cute starfish hairband is the perfect hair accessory for both grown-up and little mermaids – perhaps you could make matching hairbands together? With a cluster of glimmering starfish perched in your hair, all you must do now is decide what to wear!

Materials:

- Plain metal hairband
- Tube of two-part rapid-set epoxy glue (60–90 second setting time)
- Clear nail polish or white (PVA) craft glue
- 2 m (80 in.) piece of matte ribbon (to match your hair colour), approx. 1 cm (½ in.) wide
- 20 g (1 oz) turquoise polymer clay
- 25 ml (1 fl. oz) tube of silver acrylic paint
- 10 x 10 cm (4 x 4 in.) piece of felt (to match your hair colour)
- Sprinkle of iridescent blue glitter flakes

Equipment:

- Palette for mixing glue
- Cocktail sticks
- Scissors
- Weighing scales
- Craft mat
- Baking tray
- Oven
- Palette for paint
- Paintbrushes
- Paper
- Fine-grain sandpaper

Mermaid Tip:

Polymer clay does not air dry, but it will attract dust if it is uncovered for too long. Keep any unused clay in a sealed container and cover any sculptures which haven't been baked with an upturned bowl until they are ready to go in the oven.

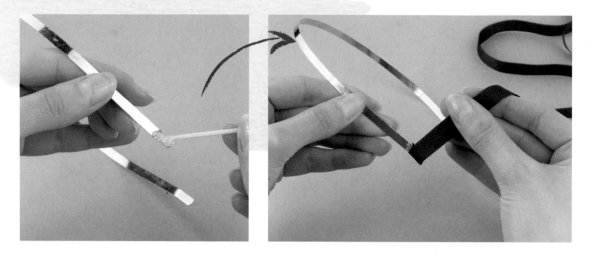

1 Mix a small amount of the two-part epoxy glue (according to the packet instructions) and use a cocktail stick to spread the glue onto one of the hairband's earpieces. Stick one end of the matt ribbon over the glue and wrap around the earpiece a few times to hide the metal. Hold the ribbon in place until the glue has set.

2 Wrap the ribbon tightly around the hairband, overlapping each layer slightly so that the metal beneath cannot be seen. (You may need to mix another small amount of glue to dot along the hairband to help keep the ribbon in place.) When the whole hairband is covered, wrap the ribbon around the other earpiece and secure in place with more freshly mixed two-part glue. Trim off the excess ribbon and fix the raw edges with clear nail polish or white (PVA) craft glue.

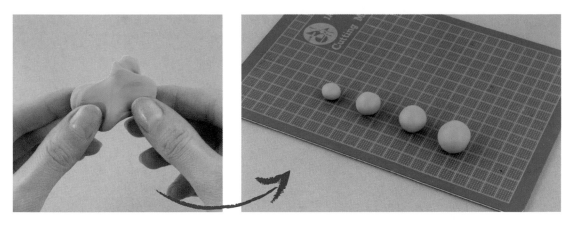

3 Knead the polymer clay in your hands for a few minutes to make it softer and more pliable – this process is known as "conditioning" and will make the clay easier to sculpt. Different brands of clay are harder than others, so don't worry if your clay takes time to soften. Divide the clay into four pieces which gradually decrease in size: 8 g, 6 g, 4 g and 2 g (¼ oz, ⅛ oz, ⅒ oz and ⅟₂₀ oz). Roll each piece into a smooth ball, either between the palms of your hands or on the surface of a craft mat.

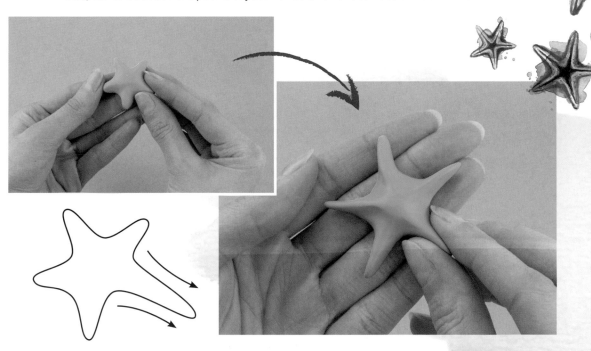

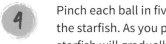

4 Pinch each ball in five equally distanced places to elongate the arms of the starfish. As you pull the arms away from the centre of the ball, the starfish will gradually flatten out into a less rounded shape.

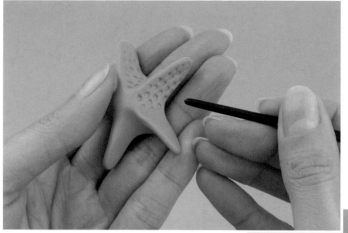

5

Use the end of a paintbrush to create a dimpled texture between the arms of each starfish, pressing gently so that you don't warp the shape of the clay.

6

Place the starfish onto a clean baking tray and bake in the oven according to the packet instructions. Leave them to cool on the tray; the clay needs to cool completely before being handled.

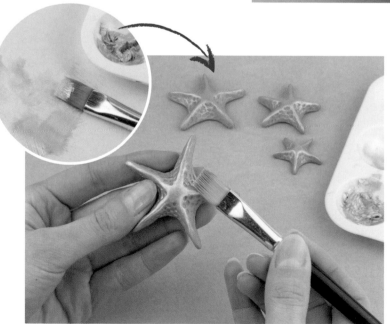

7

Dip a medium-sized paintbrush into a small amount of silver acrylic paint and dab the brush onto a plain piece of paper to remove most of the paint from the bristles. Dry brush the remaining paint over the surface of the starfish to pick out the textured detail.

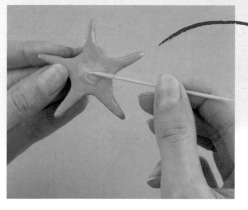

 Scuff the underside of each starfish with a piece of sandpaper to roughen the surface of the clay slightly. Mix another small amount of the two-part glue and use a cocktail stick to spread glue on the underside of the largest starfish. Stick it to the middle-side of the hairband, holding firmly in place until the glue has set. Repeat with the other starfish, spacing them approximately the same distance from one another. (Before gluing the starfish onto the hairband, you may want to temporarily tape them on with masking tape to check you are happy with the positioning.)

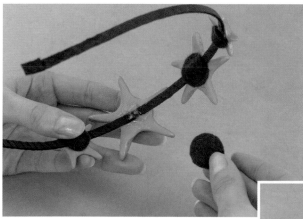

 Cut out four small circles of felt which fit over the back of each starfish. Stick each piece of felt to the underside of the hairband and onto the starfish with more freshly mixed two-part glue; this will hide the scuffed underside of the clay.

 Mix another small amount of the two-part glue and spread a very thin layer over the top of the starfish with a cocktail stick. Sprinkle glitter over the glue, then shake the hairband gently to remove any excess.

Sea Salt Bath Bombs

Pop one of these pretty bath bombs into warm, running water and enjoy a luxurious, colourful sea salt fizz! Who knew sea foam could be such fun?

Materials:

- Splash of neutral-smelling clear vegetable oil
- 340 g (12 oz) sodium bicarbonate
- 170 g (6 oz) citric acid powder
- 3 (heaped) tbsp of sea salt
- 5 ml (¼ fl. oz) bottle of purple soap dye
- 5 ml (¼ fl. oz) bottle of pink soap dye
- 5 ml (¼ fl. oz) bottle of green soap dye
- 5 ml (¼ fl. oz) bottle of coconut fragrance oil (or an essential oil of your choice)
- Small pot of biodegradable blue glitter flakes*

Equipment:

- 6 cm (2 ½ in.) diameter bath bomb mould (or a variety of different sizes and shapes!)
- Large mixing bowl
- Hand whisk or fork
- Teaspoon
- 3 small mixing bowls
- Weighing scales
- Spray bottle of water
- Metal spoon
- Plate

*As these bath bombs will eventually be washed away, it is vitally important that you use biodegradable glitter; plastic is not good for your ocean friends!

1

Grease the insides of a bath bomb mould with a small amount of clear vegetable oil – this will prevent the bath bombs from sticking to the mould.

2

Mix the sodium bicarbonate, citric acid and sea salt together in a large mixing bowl. If necessary, break up any clumps with a fork. Add approximately one teaspoon of fragrance oil to the bowl and whisk the mixture thoroughly to prevent it from clumping. Continue adding fragrance oil for a stronger scent, if desired. Divide the mixture equally between three smaller bowls.

3

Gradually add a few drops of purple soap dye to one of the bowls and whisk rapidly with a fork to prevent the mixture from fizzing. Keep adding drops of dye and whisking rapidly, until the mixture turns pale purple. Repeat this process for the other two bowls, adding green dye to one and pink dye to the other.

4

Spray each bowl of dry mixture with water, a little bit at a time, and whisk quickly to prevent the mixture from fizzing. Continue spraying the bowls with water until all three colours resemble damp sand and the mixture sticks together when compressed.

5

Combine a small amount of purple mixture with a large pinch of glitter and press into one half of the mould – mixing the glitter with a little of the bath bomb mixture will help it stick to the top of the bath bomb.

6

Continue filling both sides of the mould with layers of coloured mix, pressing the mixture firmly with your fingertips. If there are any gaps, the bath bomb may fall apart when removed from the mould.

7

When both halves of the mould are slightly overfilled, press them tightly together.

8

To remove the bath bomb, tap the mould firmly with a metal spoon a few times and then gently pull the two halves of the mould apart. Carefully lift the bath bomb from the mould and place it on a plate.

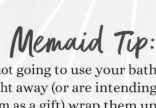

Memaid Tip:

If you are not going to use your bath bombs straight away (or are intending to give them as a gift) wrap them up in tissue paper and store them in a sealed container away from moisture. Use within a few weeks of making for the freshest scent and the best fizz!

9   Repeat Steps 5–8, until you have no more mixture left (you should be able to make at least four bath bombs from the mix). Leave the bath bombs somewhere warm to dry.

Peppermint Bath Salts

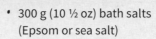

After a long, tiring day on your fins, what could be more calming than an aromatic rock pool filled with delicious peppermint scent? Sprinkle these pretty pastel salts into warm water, close your eyes and let your tail unwind.

Materials:

- 300 g (10 ½ oz) bath salts (Epsom or sea salt)
- 5 ml (¼ fl. oz) bottle of purple soap dye
- 5 ml (¼ fl. oz) bottle of green soap dye
- 5 ml (¼ fl. oz) bottle of blue soap dye
- 5 ml (¼ fl. oz) bottle of peppermint essential oil (or an essential oil of your choice)
- 3 small glass jars or bottles with airtight lids

Equipment:

- Weighing scales
- 3 small mixing bowls
- 3 forks
- Spoon

1. Divide the bath salts equally between three small mixing bowls using the weighing scales. Add few drops of soap dye to each bowl and mix with a fork. Continue adding dye and mixing thoroughly, until the salts are brightly coloured. Add a drop of peppermint essential oil (a little goes a long way!) to each bowl and stir again.

2. Leave the bath salts somewhere warm to dry and then spoon into the glass jars and seal shut. You can either mix the colours or keep them separate.

Tide Pool Treasures

Pretty trinkets for your underwater grotto!

Raindrop Moon Lantern

Raindrops and moonlight... a mermaid's delight! This beautiful moon lantern will bathe your lagoon with soft, ethereal light – just like moonlight on the waves.

Materials:

- 20 cm (8 in.) diameter paper lantern
- 8 pieces of tracing paper, approx. 30 cm high x 21 cm wide (12 in. high x 8 ½ in. wide)
- 50 ml (2 fl. oz) tube of dark blue acrylic paint
- 50 ml (2 fl. oz) tube of turquoise acrylic paint
- 50 ml (2 fl. oz) tube of pale blue acrylic paint
- 50 ml (2 fl. oz) tube of white acrylic paint
- White (PVA) craft glue
- String of 20–30 battery-powered LED fairy lights
- Small fabric bag with a draw string, slightly larger than the fairy lights' battery pack
- 1 m (39 in.) piece of silver wire, approx. 0.5–1 mm weight

Equipment:

- Tablespoon
- 4 glass jars
- Paintbrushes
- Bowl or sink of water
- Plastic tray, slightly larger than the tracing paper
- Paper towels
- Pair of compasses (or a 5 cm (2 in.) diameter cylindrical object you can draw around)
- Ruler
- Pencil
- Scissors
- Glue gun*

*If little mermaids want to try this craft, they could use quick-drying/tacky white (PVA) craft glue instead of a glue gun.

1. Start by pouring a few centimetres of each colour acrylic paint into separate glass jars. Mix the paints with a splash of water and a little white craft glue, until the paint drips easily from a brush. Dip one sheet of tracing paper into a bowl or sink of water, but don't allow it to soak for too long. Lay the tracing paper gently in a plastic tray and pat the surface with a paper towel to remove any excess water.

2. To create the darkest layer of raindrop paper, scatter diluted dark blue paint across the wet tracing paper with a medium to large paintbrush. Follow with few flecks of diluted turquoise paint, the colours should bleed together to create a rain-splattered effect. Leave the paper in the tray to dry; it may wrinkle or buckle, but this will not matter. When the paper has dried, remove from the tray and set aside for later.

3. For the next shade of raindrop paper, dip a second piece of tracing paper briefly in water and place it in the plastic tray. Blot with another paper towel to remove excess water from the surface. Drip mostly diluted turquoise paint across the paper, followed by a generous scattering of diluted pale blue paint and a few flecks of dark blue. Leave the paper in the tray to dry and then remove and set aside for later.

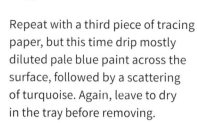

4

Repeat with a third piece of tracing paper, but this time drip mostly diluted pale blue paint across the surface, followed by a scattering of turquoise. Again, leave to dry in the tray before removing.

5

For the palest shade of raindrop paper, drip mostly diluted white paint across another sheet of wet tracing paper, followed by a scattering of pale blue or turquoise.

6

When all of the sheets of tracing paper are dry, repeat Steps 1–5 with another four pieces of tracing paper (this will ensure you have enough raindrop paper to cover the whole lantern).

Use a pair of compasses (or sketch around a cylindrical object) to draw 5 cm (2 in.) diameter circles on the non-painted side of the raindrop paper. You should be able to fit approximately 10–12 circles on each piece. Cut out the circles neatly with a pair of scissors and sort into piles of similar colours.

Glue two rings of the darkest coloured circles (paint-side facing out) around the bottom of the paper lantern with a glue gun. Dot a small amount of glue on the back of each circle and stick them to the lantern one at a time, overlapping the edges slightly to create the impression of layered scales.

Continue gluing raindrop circles to the lantern, gradually choosing lighter circles to create a gradient. Slightly overlap each layer of scales over the last to hide the paper of the lantern beneath.

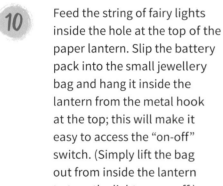

Mermaid Tip:
This craft can get very messy, so wear old clothes and cover your work surface with newspaper or a large sheet of plastic!

10   Feed the string of fairy lights inside the hole at the top of the paper lantern. Slip the battery pack into the small jewellery bag and hang it inside the lantern from the metal hook at the top; this will make it easy to access the "on-off" switch. (Simply lift the bag out from inside the lantern to turn the lights on or off.)

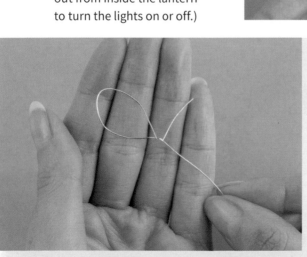

11

To hang your finished lantern, create a 2 cm (¾ in.) loop at both ends of the silver wire. Slip one loop around the metal hook at the top of the lantern.

Treasure Chest

Humans always seem to be leaving fascinating things in shipwrecks or interesting treasures on the sand! Next time you go foraging for long-lost trinkets, why not keep your favourite finds tucked away inside this mysterious treasure chest?

Materials:

- Wooden treasure chest (clasp removed), approx. 10 cm high x 16 cm wide x 11 cm deep (4 in. high x 6 ½ in. wide x 4 ½ in. deep)

- 4 small scallop shells, approx. 5 cm high x 4 cm wide (2 in. high x 1 ½ in. wide)

- 4 green shimmery glass pebbles, approx. 2 cm (¾ in.) diameter

- Tube of two-part rapid-set epoxy glue (60–90 second setting time)

- 80–100 g (3–3 ½ oz) white two-part self-hardening epoxy clay (40–50 g (1 ½–2 oz) of each part)

- 50 ml (2 fl. oz) tube of dark blue acrylic paint

- 50 ml (2 fl. oz) tube of turquoise acrylic paint

- 50 ml (2 fl. oz) tube of "antique" gold acrylic paint

- Small bottle of satin acrylic varnish

Equipment:

- Cocktail sticks

- Palette for mixing glue

- Pencil

- Paper (optional)

- Masking tape

- Craft mat

- Paintbrushes

- Small jar of water

- Palette for paint

Mix a small amount of the two-part epoxy glue and use a cocktail stick to spread the glue along the bottom inside edge of one scallop shell. Glue the shell to the middle front edge of the box lid, leaving approximately 2–3 cm (¾–1 ¼ in.) of shell hanging down over the front of the box. Hold the shell in place until the glue has set. Mix another small amount of the two-part glue and stick one glass pebble to the middle front of the box, below the edge of the shell. Leave approximately 5 mm between the pebble and the shell (this will be filled with clay later).

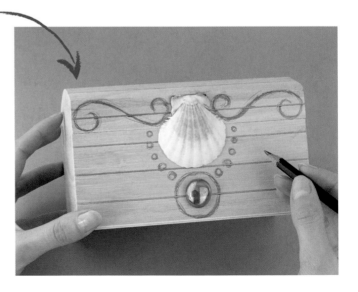

Sketch a swirling, ornate design onto the front of the box with a pencil. You can either copy the example here (see the template on page 157) or make up your own pattern.

Mix another small amount of the two-part glue and use a cocktail stick to spread the glue along the bottom inside edges of two more scallop shells. Glue one scallop shell to each side of the box, leaving approximately 2–3 cm (¾–1 ¼ in.) of shell overlapping the side of the box lid. Stick a small piece of masking tape over the shells to hold them in place until the glue dries.

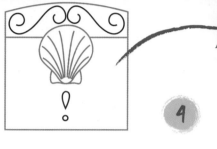

④

Sketch a symmetrical swirling design on both sides of the box, above or around the shells. You can either copy this example or make up your own design.

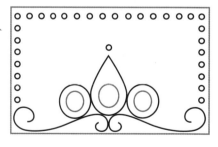

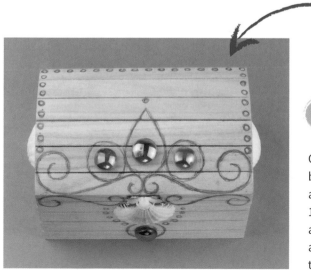

⑤

Glue three glass pebbles to the top of the box lid, approximately 1.5–2 cm (½–¾ in.) away from the edge. Leave approximately 1 cm (½ in.) space between the pebbles, as this will be filled with clay later. Sketch a design for the top of the box that frames the pebbles and the edges of the lid.

6

Thoroughly mix a small amount of the two-part epoxy clay (according to the packet instructions); it is best to mix small amounts of the clay as you need it, so that it doesn't start to harden before you have finished sculpting. Roll small balls of clay into string-like pieces, approximately 3 mm in diameter.

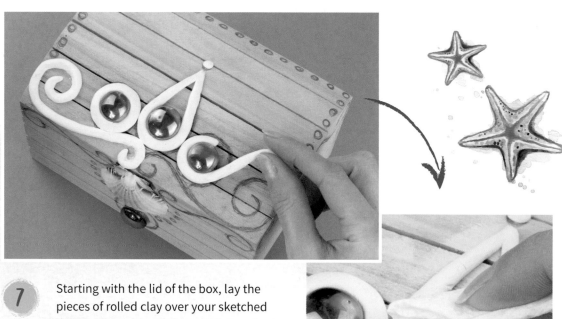

7 Starting with the lid of the box, lay the pieces of rolled clay over your sketched design and press gently to stick the clay to the surface of the lid. Use your fingertips to blend the edges of the clay onto the wood. If you smudge any clay over the glass pebbles, wipe away with the corner of a damp cloth before the clay hardens.

Mermaid Tip:

Two-part epoxy clay is self-hardening and does not need to be baked; it will harden within a few hours of mixing. Although water will smooth the surface of the clay, it will not prevent the clay from eventually setting. Often, two-part clay can be a little soft or sticky when first mixed, which can make it more difficult to sculpt. If this is the case, leave the clay for 10–15 minutes to firm-up a little before sculpting.

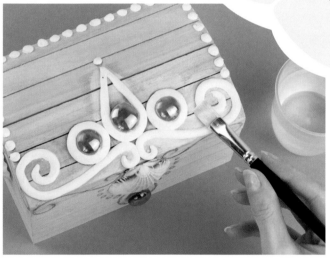

8

Smooth away any fingerprints on the surface of the clay with a paintbrush dipped in water. Leave the clay to harden (check the drying times for the brand of clay you are using) before moving on to the next side.

9

Repeat Steps 6–8 for the rest of the box, allowing plenty of drying time between each side.

10 Paint both the inside and the outside of the box in dark blue acrylic paint. This is best done one side at a time so as not to accidentally stick the lid shut! To avoid covering the pebbles with paint, use a smaller paintbrush to carefully paint around them. Depending on the thickness of the paint, you may need to cover the box in a second coat to achieve a solid colour.

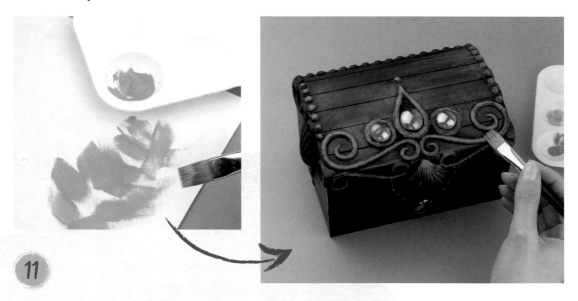

11 Dip a medium-sized paintbrush into a small amount of turquoise acrylic paint. Dab the brush onto a plain piece of paper to remove most of the paint from the bristles. Dry brush the remaining paint lightly over the surface of the whole box to pick out the texture of the wood.

Mermaid Tip:
You can use any unvarnished
wooden box for this craft, but you
may need to adapt your design
slightly to fit the dimensions of
your box. Why not experiment with
other embellishments: pieces of
driftwood, different shaped shells
or interesting colours of sea glass?

12

Use a small paintbrush to dab
antique gold paint over the
scallop shells and clay details.

13

Glaze the whole box in satin
acrylic varnish. Again, this
is best done one side at a
time so as not to accidentally
stick the lid shut!

Rock Pool Tealights

Scatter these beautiful tealights around your rock pool for a relaxing soak, bathed in a soft, warm glow. Let your worries float away as their enchanting light washes over you.

Materials:

- 10 tealight wicks with circular metal bases
- 10 small to medium cup-shaped shells (look for clam or oyster shells about the same size as a tealight)
- 130–150 g (4 ½–5 ½ oz) of white wax flakes
- 5 ml (¼ fl. oz) bottle of pink or purple liquid candle dye

Equipment:

- Knife
- Chopping board
- Heat-proof jug
- Microwave
- Spoon

1 Place one wick in the middle of each shell, ensuring that the metal bases of the wicks sit in the deepest part of the shells. Sprinkle the wax flakes into a heat-proof jug and microwave for 30 second bursts, stirring thoroughly between each. When the wax has fully melted, add a very small amount of the liquid dye and stir again. Keep adding dye until the wax reaches a pastel shade. (Melted wax will look darker than set wax.)

2 Gently pour the melted wax into each of the shells, being careful not to dislodge the wicks. Don't move the shells until the wax has set.

Marbled Mugs

Is all your crockery looking just a little bit tired and sea-worn? Why not brighten up your cups with a splash of colour? These marbled mugs are ideal if you have a mermaid friend swimming by for a cup of sea-green smoothie!

Materials:

- A selection of 5 ml (¼ fl. oz) bottles of pastel coloured nail polish (pink, blue, turquoise, purple or green)
- 2 white china mugs

Equipment:

- Sink full of soapy water
- Paper towels
- Large bowl
- Cocktail sticks
- Plastic tray

1

Clean both mugs in warm soapy water and dry thoroughly as this will ensure the polish sticks properly to the surface.

2

Fill a large bowl with warm water (cold water will actually harden nail polish faster) and leave to settle. Drip two or three colours of nail polish into the water and swirl around with a cocktail stick. The polish will start to harden shortly after pouring, so you will need to move on to the next step quickly.

3

Gently dip the bottom of one white mug into the water at a diagonal angle, until approximately 4–5 cm (1 ½–2 in.) is submerged at the deepest point. Lift the mug back out of the water, tilting it to and fro slightly to pick up the floating polish. Place the mug upside down on a plastic tray to dry.

Wash your marbled mugs gently by hand to preserve the colour. If you fancy trying a new pattern, you can easily remove the existing marbling with some acetone-based nail polish remover and re-dip the mugs in fresh polish.

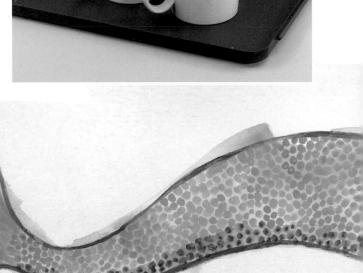

4 Scoop out any remaining pieces of nail polish and dispose of carefully before pouring away the leftover water. Refill the bowl with fresh warm water and repeat Steps 2–3 for the second mug. Leave both mugs for 24 hours to allow the nail polish to completely harden.

Seashell Fairy Lights

Materials:

- 20 cockle shells (40 matching halves)
- String of 20 LED fairy lights, batteries removed

Equipment:

- Glue gun

Bring an ocean glow to any occasion with a pretty string of enchanted seashells! Perfect as a table-topper for an Atlantean wedding, these seashell fairy lights will delight your marine guests with their soft, ethereal glow!

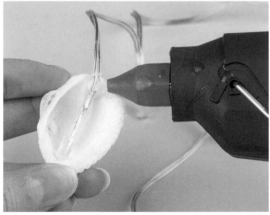

1 Start at the very end of the fairy light string, and place the last LED bulb within one of the cockle shell halves. Use a glue gun to stick the base of the bulb to the inside edge of the shell. Avoid covering the blub with glue.

2 Carefully coat the edge of the shell in a thin layer of glue; you will need to work quickly and neatly before the glue sets. Press the matching half of the shell over the glue, ensuring the pieces line up perfectly. Hold the two halves together until the glue has dried. Repeat this process for the rest of the fairy lights.

Driftwood Seahorse

Humans seem to leave shipwrecks all over the place! With plenty of driftwood to choose from, it's easy to forage for interesting shapes and colours to make this charming little seahorse.

Materials:

- Piece of card (0.5 mm weight), approx. 30 cm high x 21 cm wide (12 in. high x 8 ½ in. wide)
- 25 cm (9 in.) piece of natural string
- PVA wood glue
- Assorted driftwood

Equipment:

- Pencil
- Ruler
- Scissors
- Small jar for glue
- Paintbrushes

Mermaid Tip:

Why not try some different shapes? Dolphins, starfish or turtles are all simple variations you might like to try.

1

Start by sketching a simple 27 cm (10 in.) high seahorse outline onto the piece of card, or enlarge the template on page 156.

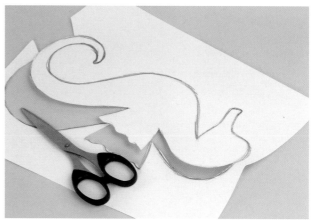

2

Cut out the seahorse with a pair of scissors; you don't have to worry about being too neat as the edges of the card will eventually be hidden under pieces of driftwood.

3

Fold the natural string in half and knot the ends together to create a loop. Glue the loop to the top of the seahorse with a small dab of wood glue and leave to dry.

4

Glue the driftwood onto the seahorse with plenty of wood glue, ensuring that the ends of wood overhang the edges of the card. This part is a bit like doing a jigsaw puzzle – you will need to sort through your collection of driftwood to find pieces that slot together in interesting ways!

5 As you gradually work down to the tail of the seahorse, angle the driftwood slightly so that it follows the curve of the tail. You will likely need to snap narrow pieces of wood into smaller lengths to fit around the smallest part of the tail.

6 When the first side of the seahorse is completely covered with driftwood, leave to dry for at least 24 hours. Repeat Steps 4–5 for the other side of the seahorse.

Ocean Ripple Cushion

On a warm summer's day, what could be better than relaxing on a cushion of comfortable ocean ripples? Stretch out your fins, sun your scales and dive into your favourite book (*The Little Mermaid*?).

Materials:

- 40 x 40 cm (15 x 15 in.) white cotton cushion cover (man-made fibres may not absorb fabric dye so well)
- 50 g (1 ¾ oz) sachet of blue fabric dye powder
- 50 g (1 ¾ oz) sachet of turquoise fabric dye powder
- 2 (heaped) tbsp salt
- 40 x 40 cm (15 x 15 in.) cushion pad

Equipment:

- Pencil
- 8 rubber bands
- Rubber gloves
- 2 squeezy bottles with nozzles, 200 ml (7 fl. oz) capacity
- Funnel
- Spoon
- Large bowl
- Plastic bag
- Scissors
- Iron and ironing board

1 Wash the cushion cover in warm soapy water, rinse well and leave damp; this will help the dye to soak into the fabric. Make a small mark in the middle of each side of the cover with a pencil.

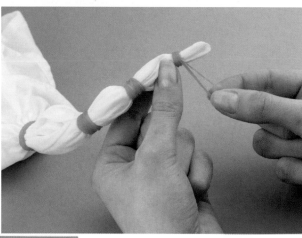

Pinch one side of the cover, where you made the pencil mark, and gather the fabric together. Tie four rubber bands tightly around the gathered fabric; the tighter the better. Leave a few centimetres between each band, but don't worry if the bands aren't evenly spaced as this will create a more natural "ripple" effect.

Pinch the other side of the cushion cover and gather the fabric together in the same way you did for the first side. Tie four more rubber bands tightly around the gathered fabric.

There are many different ways you can tie the rubber bands to create interesting patterns when tie-dying fabric. You could experiment with different tying techniques on small scrap pieces of cotton or old T-shirts.

4

Before you mix up the dye, don't forget to put rubber gloves on as fabric dye will stain skin very easily. Pour the two powdered dyes into separate squeezy bottles, using a funnel to avoid spillages. Add one heaped tablespoon of salt to each bottle and then top up both bottles with hot water.

5

Screw the nozzles onto the bottles (caps closed) and shake well to dissolve all the dye powder and salt. If the dye clumps together at the bottom of the bottles, unscrew the nozzles and stir the dye with the handle of a spoon.

6 When the dyes are thoroughly mixed, hold the cushion cover over a large bowl and squeeze the liquid generously over the fabric. Keep alternating between the two colours until there are no white areas of fabric remaining. Place the cushion cover inside a plastic bag and seal well to prevent the dye from drying out. Leave in a warm place for 48 hours to allow the dye to "fix" into the fabric.

7 Remove the cushion cover from the bag and rinse thoroughly in cold water to wash off the excess dye. Keep rinsing until the water runs clear, this may take some time. Use a pair of scissors to snip off the rubber bands, then rinse again in more cold water. Leave in a warm place to dry.

Mermaid Tip:
Always check the washing
instructions for your chosen brand
of fabric dye. If in doubt, gently
hand-wash dyed garments in cool
water to preserve the colour.

8 Iron the cover according to
temperature directions on
the label and then slip the
cushion pad inside the cover.

Deep-Sea Dreamcatcher

Curl up on your sea sponge and sink into a peaceful sleep as this dreamcatcher flutters gently in the sea breeze. With pretty peppermint ribbons drifting dreamily on the wind, you'll soon be lulled into a deep-sea slumber.

Materials:

- 40 cm (15 in.) piece of peppermint green embroidery thread
- Green glass bead, approx. 1 cm (½ in.) diameter
- Tacky white (PVA) craft glue

For the web:

- 15 cm (6 in.) diameter metal hoop
- 2 m (80 in.) piece of peppermint green ribbon, 1 cm (½ in.) wide
- 2.5 m (98 in.) piece of peppermint green embroidery thread
- Handful of assorted small pastel-coloured beads and shells (with ready-made holes), approx. 3–4 mm diameter

For the tail:

- Assorted ribbons, approx. 1 m (40 in.) long
- Assorted beads and small shells (with ready-made holes)
- 3 pieces of 50 cm (20 in.) long peppermint green embroidery thread
- 12 large turquoise flower petals

Equipment:

- Scissors
- Small paintbrush
- Pencil

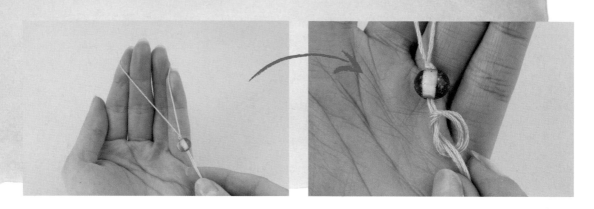

 Fold the 40 cm (15 in.) piece of peppermint green embroidery thread in half and tie in a knot approximately 8 cm (3 in.) from the ends. Slide the large green glass bead onto both ends of the thread (up to the knot) and then knot the threads again to sandwich the bead in place.

Wrap the remaining ends of the thread around the metal hoop and secure with plenty of tacky craft glue. Leave to dry before moving on to the next step.

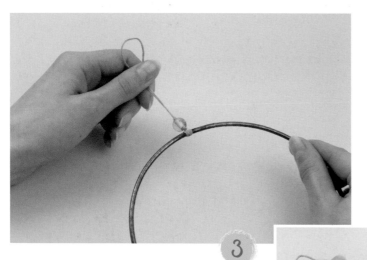

Glue one end of the 2 m (80 in.) piece of peppermint green ribbon to the top of the metal hoop, over the area where you glued the embroidery thread. When the glue has dried, wrap the ribbon tightly around the hoop at a slightly diagonal angle. When the whole hoop is covered (and you have returned to the place where you started), trim off the excess ribbon with a pair of scissors and secure the end with more tacky glue. Leave to dry before moving on to the next step.

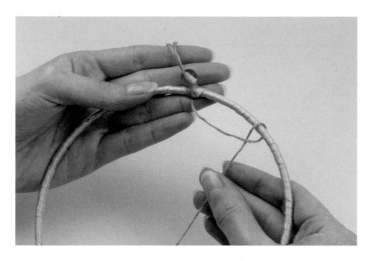

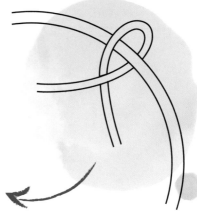

4 Tie one end of the 2.5 m (98 in.) piece of peppermint green embroidery thread to the top of the hoop and fix the knot with a dab of tacky glue. Wrap the thread over the hoop a few times to hide the knot. Moving in a clockwise direction, create one "half-hitch" knot (looping the thread over the metal hoop as pictured) approximately 4–5 cm (1 ½–2 in.) away from the top of the hoop and pull the thread taught.

5

Create seven more equally spaced half-hitch knots around the hoop, pulling the thread tightly after each knot: this will form the first layer of the web.

Mermaid Tip:

This craft is a fantastic way of using up bits and bobs of ribbon and threads from other crafts!

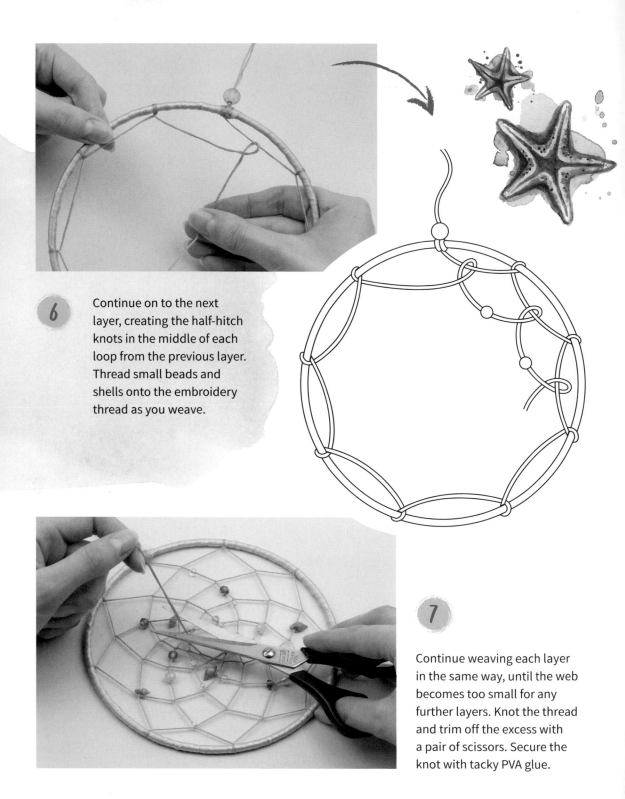

6 Continue on to the next layer, creating the half-hitch knots in the middle of each loop from the previous layer. Thread small beads and shells onto the embroidery thread as you weave.

7 Continue weaving each layer in the same way, until the web becomes too small for any further layers. Knot the thread and trim off the excess with a pair of scissors. Secure the knot with tacky PVA glue.

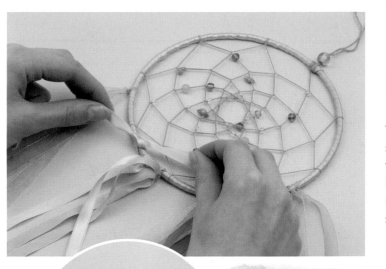

8

Tie an assortment of ribbons, strings of beads and sequins to the bottom half of the hoop. Fix the ends of the ribbons with a little glue to stop them from fraying.

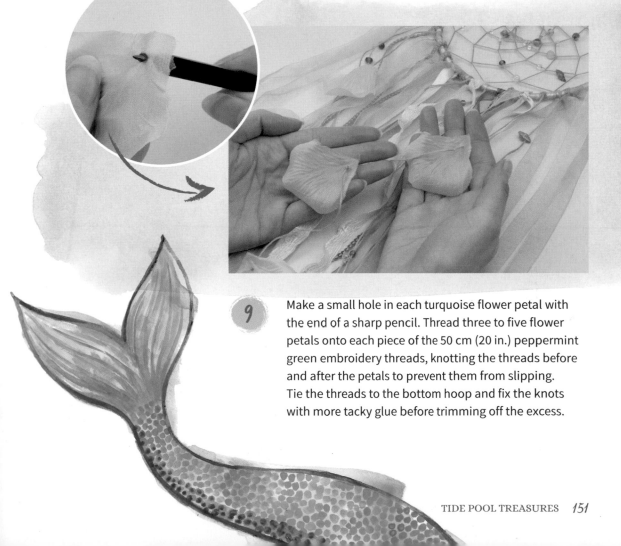

9

Make a small hole in each turquoise flower petal with the end of a sharp pencil. Thread three to five flower petals onto each piece of the 50 cm (20 in.) peppermint green embroidery threads, knotting the threads before and after the petals to prevent them from slipping. Tie the threads to the bottom hoop and fix the knots with more tacky glue before trimming off the excess.

Painted Pebbles

When the sea is too stormy for swimming, and small fry are looking for something to do, why not fill your ocean grotto with some pretty painted pebbles? Little mermaids will love painting these stones and they will bring a pop of colour to a grey day!

Materials:

- Handful of large pebbles, approx. 5–6 cm (2–2 ½ in.) diameter
- 50 ml (1 ¾ fl. oz) tubes of bright pastel acrylic paints (pink, green, purple, blue)
- Small bottle of satin acrylic varnish

Equipment:

- Paintbrushes
- Palette for paint

1 Paint each pebble in an even layer of acrylic paint, one side at a time. Depending on the thickness of the paint, you may need to coat the pebbles in a second layer to achieve a solid colour. Leave to dry before moving on to the next step.

2 Use a small to medium paintbrush to dot, swirl or splatter contrasting coloured paint across the pebbles. Be creative – it is up to you what patterns you make! When you have finished painting the pebbles, leave to dry.

3 Glaze both sides of the pebbles with satin acrylic varnish, leaving plenty of drying time between each side.

Acknowledgements

Firstly, I would like to thank "my mermaids": Kelly Feng, Amber De-Terville, Rosie James, Rosalind Thompson and Alissa Thompson. You are all lovely, kind-hearted people and I am so grateful you could all flip your fins down to the beach to model my crafts.

Thank you to my "umbrella holders": Jacqui Thompson and Robert Wills. You both held that umbrella so patiently while I took "just one more" photograph.

Thank you to Blake Troise for continually assuring me that mermaids would like these crafts, and for encouraging me to just get on and write this book. I am sorry our house is now full of "mermaid stuff" and the carpets are all covered in fabric dye.

Thank you to Imi Hart, for listening to me talk incessantly (at you) about this book, often until 4 a.m., and over many cups of tea.

Thank you to Christie Bell for being both a fantastic ballet teacher and a wonderful friend, and for listening to my hopes for this book during our "after-class chats".

And finally, thank you to Faye Lewis, Kate Cooper, Rita Eccles, Anna Martin, Chris Turton, Debbie Chapman, Hannah Adams, Ken McKay, Claire Plimmer, Alastair Williams, Charlotte Williams and the rest of Summersdale Publishers for believing in my passion for mermaids!

About the Author

Marianne Charlotte Thompson is an artist and designer who loves the sound of falling rain, the feel of new sketchbooks and all things fairy tale themed. When she isn't at her easel painting (another mermaid or fairy!), she is dancing, swimming or endlessly searching for the perfect piece of sea glass. Her love of mermaids began as a small child and intensified after many glorious summers spent swimming or rock pooling on the beautiful Isle of Wight beaches.

www.mariannecharlotteart.com

www.facebook.com/mariannecharlotteart

www.twitter.com/MCT_art
(@MCT_art)

www.instagram.com/mariannecharlotteart/
(@mariannecharlotteart)

Useful Templates

Enlarge these templates on your scanner or photocopier.

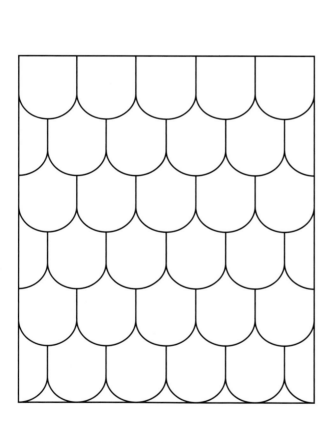

Splattered Scales Tote Bag (p.54)

Driftwood Seahorse (p.136)

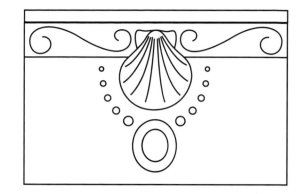

Treasure Chest (p.120)

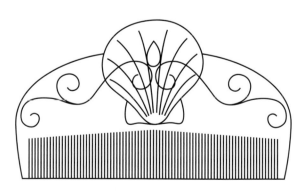

Scallop Shell Shirt (p.14)

Golden Comb (p.88)

Mermaiding Resources

Swimmable mermaid tails, accessories and monofins

Merbella Studios:
www.shopmerbella.com

Finfolk Productions:
www.finfolkproductions.com

Mertailor:
www.themertailor.com

The MerNation:
www.themernation.com

Planet Mermaid:
www.planetmermaid.com

Swim Tails:
www.swimtails.com

Finis:
www.finisswim.com

The Mermaid Cave:
www.the-mermaid-cave.co.uk

Fin Fun:
www.finfunmermaid.com

Inspiring professional mermaids

Mermaid Kariel:
www.mermaidkariel.com

Hannah Mermaid:
www.hannahmermaid.com

Mermaid Melissa:
www.mermaidmelissa.com

Raina Mermaid:
www.mermaidraina.com

Mermaid Syrena:
www.themermaidsyrena.com

Mermaid Hyli:
www.facebook.com/MerHyli

Helena the Mermaid:
www.facebook.com/HelenaTheMermaid

Mermaid schools and swim lessons

Sirenas Mediterranean Academy (Spain):
www.sirenasmediterraneanacademy.com

Aqua Mermaid (USA, Canada & Mexico):
www.aquamermaid.com

Mermaid Kat Academy (Australia):
www.mermaidacademy.com.au

Philippine Mermaid Swimming Academy (The Philippines):
www.philippinemermaid
swimmingacademy.com

Mayim Mermaid Academy (UK):
www.mayimmermaidacademy.co.uk

Mermaids Swim (UK & Europe):
www.mermaidsswimuk.co.uk

Meermin School (The Netherlands):
www.meerminschool.nl

Swimolino (Germany):
www.swimolino.de

South Coast Mermaids (UK):
www.southcoastmermaids.com

Mermaid performances, events and festivals

March of the Mermaids (UK):
www.facebook.com/mermaids.march

Sandy Fins (USA):
www.sandyfins.com

Weeki Wachee Mermaids (USA):
www.weekiwachee.com/mermaids

Mermaid Parade (USA):
www.coneyisland.com/programs/
mermaid-parade

Mermaid MagFest (USA):
www.mermaidmegafest.com

Merfolk UK:
www.merfolkuk.com

The Mermates (Belgium):
www.the-mermates.com

Mermaid FinFest (US):
www.mermaidfinfest.com

The California Mermaid Convention (US):
www.californiamermaidcon.com

Mermaid Dream Retreat (Mexico):
www.mermaiddreamretreats.com

Mer-community

MerNetwork:
www.mernetwork.com

MerDirectory:
www.merdirectory.com

Mermaids of Facebook:
www.facebook.com/groups/VirtualMermaids/

MERMAIDS:
www.facebook.com/groups/217230798290675/

Everything Mermaid:
www.everythingmermaid.com

Mermaid Magazine:
www.themermaidmagazine.com

Instagram hashtags:
#mermaidlife
#mermaidlifestyle
#mermaidtail
#mermaiding

Books and films

The Little Mermaid (1989)

The Little Mermaid (2018)

Splash (1984)

Pirates of the Caribbean: On Stranger Tides (2011)

Aquamarine (2006)

Ponyo (2010)

The Little Mermaid
(by Hans Christian Andersen, 1837)

Mermaids: The Myths, Legends and Lore
(by Skye Alexander, 2012)

The Mermaid Handbook
(by Carolyn Turgeon, 2018)

The Mermaid Cookbook (by Alix Carey, 2018)

If you're interested in finding out more about our books, find us on Facebook at *Summersdale Publishers* and follow us on Twitter at @*Summersdale*.

www.summersdale.com